Varieties of

LEARNING ABOUT LANGUAGE

General Editors:
Geoffrey Leech & Mick Short, Lancaster University

Varieties of Modern English

An Introduction

Diane Davies

PEARSON

Longman

Harlow, England • London • New York • Boston • San Francisco • Toronto • Sydney • Singapore • Hong Kong
Tokyo • Seoul • Taipei • New Delhi • Cape Town • Madrid • Mexico City • Amsterdam • Munich • Paris • Milan

PEARSON EDUCATION LIMITED

Edinburgh Gate
Harlow CM20 2JE
United Kingdom
Tel: +44 (0)1279 623623
Fax: +44 (0)1279 431059
Website: www.pearsoned.co.uk

First edition published in Great Britain in 2005

© Pearson Education Limited 2005

The right of Diane Davies to be identified as author
of this work has been asserted by her in accordance
with the Copyright, Designs and Patents Act 1988.

ISBN 0 582 36996 7

British Library Cataloguing in Publication Data
A CIP catalogue record for this book can be obtained from the British Library

Library of Congress Cataloging-in-Publication Data
Davies, Diane.
  Varieties of modern English / Diane Davies.
    p. cm. — (Learning about language)
  Includes bibliographical references and index.
  ISBN 0–582–36996–7 (pbk.)
  1. English language—Variation. 2. English language—Usage. I. Title. II. Series.
  PE1074.7.D38 2005
  427—dc22
                                                                            2004063322

10   9   8   7   6   5   4   3   2   1
09   08   07   06   05

Set by 35 in 10/12.5pt Palatino
Printed in Malaysia (CTP-VVP)

The Publisher's policy is to use paper manufactured from sustainable forests.

Contents

Contents

Preface

In this book I aim to provide an introduction to varieties of English for those following university or college courses in English language studies, the sociolinguistics of English, and related fields. Students of English language and literature should also find the book relevant, since a number of the textual examples I discuss in it are from literary writings. As some of the illustrative material comes from the British cultural context, the book may have a particular appeal to those interested in British English (whether as a first, second or foreign language). However, it also looks at other major varieties of English, their characteristics, users and uses.

Readers do not need prior knowledge of linguistics or methods of linguistic analysis to follow the text. However, to provide the necessary orientation, Chapter 1 gives an introduction to the study of language variation. This is followed in Chapter 2 by a brief overview of the kinds of descriptive tools needed to explore variation in more detail. Chapter 3 looks at the history of Modern English, while Chapters 4 and 5 consider respectively the global perspective on English and selected ethnic varieties of the language. Moving on to a specific dimension of user-related variation, Chapter 6 explores theories of language, gender and sexuality in relation to English. Chapter 7 discusses medium-related variation (including the use of electronic media), while Chapters 8 and 9 are both concerned with the study of English in particular contexts. Finally, Chapter 10 evaluates some of the current issues and debates in the development of English as an international language.

Overall, the book is designed to function as a general course text, covering the main topics relevant to modules on varieties of English. Ideally, the chapters are meant to be read in numerical sequence, but they could be read in a different order to suit the emphases of particular courses. The end-of-chapter Activities are intended to encourage the reader to explore the topics in more detail. They range from short exercises on the formal features of texts to ideas for small-scale research. Comments on the Activities are provided at the end of the book, giving either quite detailed suggested answers or brief, general advice.

Diane Davies
Kibworth Beauchamp, England
2004

Acknowledgements

I am indebted, first and foremost, to Geoffrey Leech for the expert advice and guidance he has given me throughout, not forgetting his patience and good humour when progress was slow. I also extend my thanks to Mick Short for his invaluable feedback on both my early plans and the final draft. It would be hard to find two more helpful and motivating editors. Thanks are also due to Casey Mein and Benjamin Roberts at Pearson for so skilfully steering the book towards publication.

I am grateful to my colleagues in the School of Education at the University of Leicester, and especially to Pamela Rogerson-Revell, Peter Martin and the staff of CELTEAL, for their support and encouragement since I joined them in 2001. My former colleagues and students at the University of Exeter (many now living and working in other places) also deserve my thanks, in particular those who provided helpful comments and newspaper cuttings.

A number of friends are owed my appreciation for helping me complete what I set out to do. My special thanks are due to Natasha Shugaeva for offering her support and practical help so generously at all times. And, for encouraging me from the earliest days of this project and often being a source of inspiration, I am also grateful to Ingrid Fischböck.

My final acknowledgement must be to my parents, Cliff and Glenys Davies, for everything they have done to ease the journey of this book, which I dedicate to them.

Publisher's acknowledgements

The publishers are grateful to the following for permission to reproduce copyright material:

'We do not play on graves', reprinted by permission of the publishers and the Trustees of Amherst College from THE POEMS OF EMILY DICKINSON: READING EDITION, edited by Ralph W. Franklin, Cambridge, Mass.: The Belknap Press of Harvard University Press. Copyright © 1998, 1999 by the President and Fellows of Harvard College. Copyright © 1951, 1955, 1979, 1983 by the President and Fellows of Harvard College; 'Jackdaw: Changes to the English language in the European Union', by Emily Sheffield, 13 June 1996, copyright © Guardian Newspapers Limited 1996; 'Jackdaw: The Essential Guide to the Southern States of America', by Desmond Christy, 30 April 1996, copyright © Guardian Newspapers Limited 1996; 'Just hanging on the telephone', by Sarah Boseley, 9 January 2001, copyright © Guardian Newspapers Limited 2001; 'Modern Recipes No: 21', by David Bennun, 7 February 1997, copyright © Guardian Newspapers Limited 1997; Bloodaxe Books for 'seasons' by Jean 'Binta' Breeze, *The Arrival of Brighteye and Other Poems* (Bloodaxe Books, 2000); Tony Harrison for 'The Queen's English'; John Sutherland for 'How the potent language of civic life was undermined', featured in *The Guardian*, 20 March 2001; excerpt from DEATH OF A SALESMAN by Arthur Miller, copyright 1949, renewed © 1977 by Arthur Miller. Used by permission of Viking Penguin, a division of Penguin Group (USA) Inc.

In some instances we have been unable to trace the owners of copyright material, and we would appreciate any information that would enable us to do so.

Chapter 1

Setting Out

1.1 Introduction

The English language varies in a number of ways, depending on the people who use it and on how, in what circumstances and why it is used. The central concern of this book is to introduce some of the key terms and concepts for studying variation related to both *users* and *uses*, as well as to illustrate and discuss particular varieties of English. It is not an assumption that you will necessarily have much knowledge at this stage of either how to analyse language in a formal sense (describing its sounds, words and sentences) or of how to talk about it from a sociolinguistic point of view (how it relates to society). Of course, what you already know about these things if you are, for example, a speaker of English as a foreign language, a student of anthropology, or someone who is bilingual, will certainly be helpful to you. What this first chapter aims to do is outline how variation is fundamental to how we use language, both as individuals and members of communities.

From one point of view, a language is a complex system of rules relating to sounds, words, sentences and the ways in which these elements are normally combined. The traditional approach to linguistics was to focus almost entirely on the forms or structures of language, whereas today there is far more emphasis on how and why people use language in particular ways, and on the dynamic interrelationship between language and communicative function. Very influential work was done on functions of language in the first half of the 20th century by, notably, the Prague Linguistic Circle (a linguistic and literary movement founded in 1926), by Bühler (1934) and Jakobson (1960). However, it is the work of linguists such as William Labov (e.g. 1972), Douglas Biber (e.g. 1988) and Michael Halliday (e.g. 1973, 1994) that has, arguably, had the greatest impact on the study of communicative function and variation in English. Halliday describes three interrelated functions (or **metafunctions**) of language: the *ideational* function of representing experience; the *interpersonal* function of expressing the relations between, and the attitudes of, the people interacting; and the *textual* function of making words and sentences into coherent text. This functional approach to language, the theoretical basis of Halliday's *systemic functional grammar*, provides a necessary bridge between language seen as an abstract system of rules and language in communicative and contextualised use. It therefore helps us to see how metafunctional variables will have some effect on the linguistic and pragmatic choices we make in any interaction, be it a routine chat with a colleague, a phone call to an insurance company, or an email message.

The distinction between form and function is also important in another way. Consider, for a moment, the possible communicative functions of the simple clause *it's raining*. Depending entirely on the context and other factors such as the speaker's intonation, the function of this sentence might be at least any of the following: social or phatic (to avoid an awkward silence); recording (to give factual information in answer to a direct question about the weather); reasoning (to explain why you don't want to go out) or emotional (to express surprise or disbelief). In other words, there is no one-to-one correlation between a declarative sentence and the function of 'declaring' something. Likewise, there is no guarantee that the communicative function of an interrogative form is necessarily to ask for information (the function of *Are you kidding?* may be to express mocking disbelief) or that the function of an imperative form is necessarily to give a command (for example, *Come round later* is likely to be taken as an informal invitation). Of course, 'knowing' a language well (whether it's a first or second language) means being aware of how its different grammatical forms may be used to 'realise' a range of communicative aims, so this is something that speakers must acquire naturally or 'learn'. Either way, in face-to-face communication in particular, there are a number of additional factors we can take into account that play a part in conveying a speaker's meaning, including the loudness and pitch of their voice, their facial expression, degree of eye contact, and their apparent feelings, moods and attitudes.

1.2　Variation and the individual

Looking at form versus function is one way of seeing how variation is part of the language we use, but there are more fundamental ways of accounting for variation than this. First, the speakers of a language do not all use it in the same way, even if they are very alike in knowledge of the language, social and regional background, and so on. Each of us has our own *verbal repertoire* or range of speech styles to draw on in particular situations. We might be very familiar with another person's speech, but we are rarely able to guess exactly what they might say in a given context, or how they might say it. Indeed, it would be the stuff of nightmares if people really did use language in exactly the same ways as each other, since this would challenge the very nature of our sense of individual differences. We only have to think of the mechanical, single-style speech of many of the most sinister inventions of science fiction, such as the Daleks in the TV series *Dr Who*, to be reminded of this.

Often the characteristics of an individual's speech are singled out for special attention. This can be seen in countless literary works, especially in drama and fiction, where particular characters are given marked speech styles to make them more distinctive or memorable. Examples include Alfred Jingle's tendency to speak 'telegraphically' in Dickens's *The Pickwick Papers*; Jay Gatsby's fondness for addressing his confidant Nick Carraway as 'old sport' in Fitzgerald's *The Great Gatsby*; and the repeated use of clichés and idioms by the isolated and self-deluding narrators of Alan Bennett's TV monologues *Talking Heads*.

Attention is also drawn to individual speech in other contexts, with the usage of politicians and celebrities often being the focus of interest, amusement or even intervention. On becoming Prime Minister of Britain, Margaret Thatcher was apparently advised to speak with a lower voice pitch, so as to sound less 'feminine' and more authoritarian (and recordings show that her speech did gradually change in this way). Another example is a billboard advertisement for Nescafé that I noticed several years ago, which represented orthographically (i.e. through spelling) the characteristic lisp of the British former boxer Chris Eubank. At the time Eubank was well known not only for this minor speech defect (accompanied by an aspiring 'upper-class' accent and fastidious choice of words) but also for a flamboyant style of dress. The poster called up these associations by showing him smartly attired in an elegant drawing room while savouring the aroma of a cup of Nescafé, accompanied by the caption 'Thimply the betht' (for 'Simply the best'). Here was a case of an individual's speech being cleverly exploited to invest a simple, everyday product with a mock-serious glamour intended to appeal to the target audience.

The individual way in which each of us speaks is called our *idiolect*, and it is a combination of the ways in which we use the sounds, words and grammar of the language. Our idiolect is not a fixed phenomenon, as our language changes according to our age and the circumstances of our lives. When I was a child there were stronger features of a Welsh accent in my English speech than there are now, although this change is largely because I have spent many years living and working outside Wales. When I was a teenager I also used different slang expressions from those I use now, and the normal pitch of my voice was probably higher. Today I regularly use the vocabulary associated with the study and teaching of English and linguistics, whereas if I went to work for a charity like Oxfam, for instance, I would start to use that of international aid agencies and human rights on a daily basis. Our idiolect is limited by what parts of the language we actually use or have access to, not just by the way we use the language.

For example, one person might be able to talk with experts on nuclear physics, another on ballet or chess. Obviously no speaker knows *all* of the language in *all* of its possible forms and contexts of use.

As individual speakers we can be very creative in our use of language (we can put on accents, invent nonsense words, create puns and language jokes, etc.). However, there is a limit to the kinds of variation we can introduce if we want to communicate clearly. As we acquire knowledge of how our language works – the rules of its interrelated systems of sounds, words and grammar – we develop an understanding of its norms and possibilities and of what type of creativity is open to us without making our speech incomprehensible. For example, we know that the sequence *They holiday on going are tomorrow* does not constitute the kind of variation in word order that standard varieties of the English language normally show, so this kind of variation is avoided. Similarly, we know that there are limits to the variations in the way words are pronounced. We might pronounce 'dog' in a range of accents (as 'dawg' or even 'dock', for instance) and remain comprehensible in context, but we know that pronouncing it as 'dot' is not really an option, because a final 't' sound is never a variant of a final 'g' in English.

When we consider variation in individual speech, we should not, however, see the individual in total isolation from other speakers. The kinds of variation possible in our speech are related not so much to abstract norms of the language as to those of the particular communities and groups to which we belong and with which we usually communicate. In the next section we will look more closely at variation from the point of view of such groups.

1.3 Variation and the group

A few years ago the case of an elderly Hungarian psychiatric patient released from many years' incarceration in Russia following the Second World War drew attention to the need we all have to be with others who speak our language. It was hoped that the man, who was unable to say who he was and had virtually stopped speaking altogether, would regain his speech on hearing his native language being spoken around him once again. Indeed, very soon after his release, TV news reports showed him once again happily conversing in Hungarian. Although an extreme case, this does suggest that the functionality and versatility of our speech even as adults tend to be closely bound up with the opportunities we have to use our language interactively. If we are denied such a possibility, the scope of our speech may become seriously limited since we will not be able to draw in the normal way on our verbal repertoire.

Most of us would accept that we use our language in a wide range of situations and with a number of other speakers on a regular basis. We might even use more than one language in this way or sometimes draw on two or more languages at the same time if we happen to share those languages with specific people. Usually linguists use the word *code* to describe the particular language, dialect or variety we choose to use on any occasion. In bilingual or multilingual communities one of the most important kinds of variation is known as **code-switching**, defined by Trudgill (2003:23) as 'a process whereby bilingual or bidialectal speakers switch back and forth between one language or dialect and another within the same conversation'. Switching may come about because one language or dialect is associated with a particular communicative domain (such as the home or when speaking about informal topics) and the other language or dialect with different domains (such as more formal, official or ceremonial contexts). In some parts of the world, like Hong Kong, Malta and Nigeria, the process may go beyond switching of this kind to **code-mixing**, where speakers use different languages even within single utterances. Trudgill (2003:23) notes that 'it is not really possible to say at any given time which language they are speaking', adding that '[s]ociolinguistic explanations for this behaviour normally concentrate on the possibility, through using code-mixing as a strategy, of projecting two identities at once, for example that of a modern, sophisticated, educated person *and* that of a loyal, local patriot [. . .]'.

The important link between language and identity (or identities) means that when we explore variation in the language used by groups of speakers, we need first to consider what we understand by 'group'. Sociolinguists often make use of the term **speech community** to describe a group of speakers who share the same language varieties or speech repertoires. On a basic level, all speakers of English belong to an English speech community, but a definition as broad as this is obviously not very useful to us in studying variation within English, since it is too all-encompassing and assumes that English is used uniformly around the globe. In reality speakers of English can be distinguished regionally, ethnically and socially, as well as through factors like their gender, jobs and interests. In other words, they belong to several speech communities at the same time, which may be discrete or intersecting. In this sense the concept of the speech community is a 'fuzzy' one, and some sociolinguists, notably Lesley Milroy and James Milroy in their research in Belfast, have preferred to adopt the anthropological concept of the **social network** in investigating the linguistic behaviour of different social groups. Lesley Milroy (1980) argues that a social network may be 'dense', depending on the extent to which the individuals in the network all know each other, and 'multiplex' to the extent that they are linked in more than one way, for example, through being relatives *and* friends *and* colleagues. Density and multiplexity thus determine *network* *strength*, and this in turn can be an important influence on group linguistic behaviour.

1.4   Dialects and accents

Dialect is popularly thought to be a use of the words and grammar of a language that can be distinguished from a supposed non-dialectal norm that is usually considered superior. It is also popularly assumed that only some of us actually use dialect. In fact we all speak a dialect, because we all use the words and sentences of English in particular ways, whether we use a standard variety of the language or not. Within England, Standard English is normally defined as the dialect of English taught in schools and to learners of the language, used in print and spoken by the most educated and powerful people. It is not (by most academic linguists) regarded as superior *linguistically* to other dialects, but since it is associated with power and success, it is obviously the most important and prestigious dialect. As we shall see in Chapter 3, the fact that one dialect of English in England became the standard dialect and the norm for dictionaries, grammar books and the teaching of the language was the result not of the intrinsic qualities of that dialect but of the fact that it was being used by the right people in the right places at the right time. It is also important to remember that, although institutionalised through being established as a standard dialect, this well-known variety of English has not remained the same throughout its history. Within Britain and North America alone it has been continually influenced by political developments and by changing debates on the choice and role of a standard dialect. And because English was destined to travel much further around the globe than any other language in history, Standard English today can be subdivided into a number of international 'Englishes', such as Standard American English or Standard Indian English.

Traditional dialects, those associated with the more remote, rural areas, together with the accents that accompany them, are now declining fast in Britain, especially in England. These dialects are being overtaken by modern dialects associated with urban centres such as London and Liverpool. The main reason for this is the decline in the sort of traditional country life that kept people isolated from the influence of the cities – a change brought about through technological advances, the expansion of education for all and the growing need for a more mobile and more educated workforce. Traditional dialects can still be heard, however, especially among older speakers who have remained in one area all their lives, as well as in some other contexts. For example, Tony Beard, a popular presenter on the local BBC radio station 'Radio Devon', uses broad Devonshire dialect in his request show and typically says things like *Us wants to wish her a happy birthday*. In this context the use of a traditional dialect can be favourably perceived by listeners as an assurance, perhaps, that their local community remains distinctive and special.

Traditional dialects are linguistically conservative and differ markedly from one another and from Standard English or modern urban varieties. While modern dialects can have a variant form like *she aint going* for *she isn't going*, traditional dialects such as those of the English West Country use forms like *her bain't a-goin* or *she byun't a-goin*. Also, certain pronunciations can be found in traditional dialects that do not occur in modern dialects, such as the pronunciation of *farmer* as 'varmer', of *long* as 'lang' and of *bone* as 'ben'.

It is not only the case that we all speak a dialect of the language but also that we pronounce it in a particular way and so also speak with an accent. This may indicate to others where we are from or what our social background is, what sort of education we have had and so on. Our accents frequently adjust in various ways to those of people from other regions and backgrounds. Someone with a strong regional accent in childhood is still unlikely, however, to lose all traces of that accent in later life (even if they try hard to), since the way we learn to pronounce our native dialect or language is both too automatic and too intricate. This is why people who learn a foreign language, even those long resident in a country where it is spoken, generally speak it with at least some of the pronunciation features of their first language.

1.4.1 Social class and English

Today in the British Isles people speak Standard English with a wide range of regional accents, though a small minority (less than 3 per cent) speak it with an accent called **RP** (*Received Pronunciation*), variously referred to during the first half of the 20th century as 'King's English', Queen's English' and 'BBC English'. RP is often defined as 'non-regional' but is nevertheless associated in most people's minds with England and particularly southern England. Speakers of RP tend to have been educated at prestigious independent schools (especially the traditional 'public schools' of Eton, Harrow and Winchester, etc.) and to belong to the most privileged socio-economic groups.

It is important to note that the differences between the varieties of English used at the extreme ends of the social spectrum can be distinguished through grammar and lexis as well as pronunciation, and that the grammatical differences are less mobile. When the Cockney flower-girl Eliza Doolittle in George Bernard Shaw's play *Pygmalion* is taught the accent of the English upper class by the phonetician Professor Henry Higgins, she successfully changes her pronunciation but continues to reveal her true origins through her grammar and choice of vocabulary, as shown in the following extract from the play, where she has just been introduced to an upper-class family:

MRS EYNSFORD HILL I'm sure I hope it wont[1] turn cold. Theres so much influenza about. It runs right through our whole family regularly every spring.

LIZA [*darkly*] My aunt died of influenza: so they said.

MRS EYNSFORD HILL [*clicks her tongue sympathetically*]!!!

LIZA [*in the same tragic tone*] But it's my belief they done the old woman in.

MRS HIGGINS [*puzzled*] Done her in?

LIZA Y-e-e-e-es, Lord love you! Why should she die of influenza? She come through diphtheria right enough the year before. I saw her with my own eyes. Fairly blue with it, she was. They all thought she was dead; but my father he kept ladling gin down her throat til she came to so sudden that she bit the bowl off the spoon.

MRS EYNSFORD HILL [*startled*] Dear me!

LIZA [*piling up the indictment*] What call would a woman with that strength in her have to die of influenza? What become of her new straw hat that should have come to me? Somebody pinched it; and what I say is, them as pinched it done her in.

MRS EYNSFORD HILL What does doing her in mean?

(George Bernard Shaw, 1916 *Pygmalion* London: Penguin)

The socially telling grammatical features of Eliza's English here include the use of present tense for past in 'She <u>come</u> through diphtheria right enough the year before' and 'What <u>become</u> of her new straw hat that should have come to me?'; the use of the past participle for the past form in 'they done the old woman in'; doubling of the subject of the clause in '<u>My father</u> <u>he</u> kept . . .'; the use of the adjective instead of the adverb in 'she came to so <u>sudden</u>', and the non-standard construction of the relative clause in 'them as pinched it'. Other revealing features would include the inversion of subject and complement in 'Fairly blue with it, she was' and the exclamation 'Lord love you!', since these are likely to have been regarded as unladylike at the time. Finally, the colloquialisms of 'done her in' (for 'murdered') and 'pinched' (for 'stolen') reinforce the mismatch between Eliza's graceful appearance, 'impeccable' accent and her self-expression.

Shaw's *Pygmalion* was first performed in English in 1914, and the social divide between accents in England was certainly more marked then than it is today. Shaw was sensitive, however, to the fact that the forms used by influential or admired speakers could be deliberately adopted by those wishing to associate with them. Ironically, soon after the extract quoted above, he deliberately inverts the usual direction of this imitation (i.e. the poorer classes wishing to imitate the better-off) and has his younger upper-

---

[1] Shaw wished to simplify the spelling rules of English, as can be seen in this passage in the deliberately simplified *wont*, *Theres* and *til*.

class characters assume that the charming Miss Doolittle is speaking not her Cockney dialect, but a new and more liberated 'small talk' that they should themselves immediately try to adopt.

These days, RP speakers are not automatically considered by speakers of English in England to speak 'better' English than those with other accents (as they were in Shaw's day). While studies have shown that RP speakers tend to be rated as more intelligent, industrious and self-confident than those with regional accents, non-RP speakers are often perceived more positively in England according to such criteria as assumed trustworthiness, warmth or sense of humour. As a socially prestigious accent, RP in England is fast losing ground to more fashionable urban accents spoken increasingly by a less deferential younger and professional generation.

1.4.2 'Estuary English'

The most frequently discussed development in recent decades with regard to the growth of British urban dialect areas has been the expansion of the London-based dialect into an extended Home Counties Modern Dialect area.[2] The accent associated with this area was termed *Estuary English* (after the Thames Estuary) by the phonetician David Rosewarne (1994), but the phenomenon has in fact spread far beyond this area. The label is described by Trudgill (1999:80) as referring to 'lower middle-class accents, as opposed to working-class accents, of the Home Counties Modern Dialect area'. Its main features are the south-east of England pronunciation of *meal* as if spelled 'meaw' and the 'swallowing' of the 't' in words like *right* and *Gatwick* (technically, the accent uses a so-called *glottal stop* for the 't', which we will learn more about in Chapter 2). *Estuary* avoids stronger Cockney features, however, such as the glottal stop before a vowel in *water* (as if spelled *wa'er*) or the pronunciation of *thing* as 'fing' or *brother* as 'bruvver'. The importance of this accent is the result of a combination of factors, including the large population base in the south-east, its frequent use by popular presenters on national TV and radio, and the upward social mobility of people from lower middle-class backgrounds in the south-east into more influential social positions. While *Estuary* is welcomed by some commentators as the accent of a less class-conscious English society, it remains to be seen how far up the social scale its influence will reach. Although some glottal stops may now be found in the speech of younger royals and upper-class speakers, suggesting the downward mobility of *their* accents, it would be unwise to conclude that these relatively 'sheltered' networks were intending to adopt wholesale the demotic speech patterns of London and the Home Counties.

---

[2] This is paralleled by the growth of some totally new dialect areas based on urban centres in other parts of the country, such as the West Midlands (centred on Birmingham), Merseyside (around Liverpool) and Humberside in NE England.

Their tendency to speak less carefully and less formally than their parents is really no different from the tendency of most younger speakers of English to adopt the accent and speech styles associated with fashionable youth culture rather than those of the older generation. While the fact that these adjustments happen at all may reflect the trend away from RP as an accent to emulate, it does not necessarily indicate that socio-economically privileged speakers will eventually lose the accent that distinguishes them from others. Accent, after all, is one of the main ways in which speakers of English with the highest social status (in England at least) have traditionally conveyed their elitism. As long as they continue to want to do so, their accent will remain identifiable and distinct from the accents of other social groups.

1.4.3 Dialect and solidarity

I shall bring this section on socio-economic class and English to a close by turning to a poem by a contemporary British poet that can in some ways be interpreted as a reflection on the gulf between standard and non-standard dialects, in this case also a gulf between a working-class father and his better-educated son. The poem uses two linguistic codes to enact the sense of dislocation that both seem to experience:

The Queen's English

Last meal together, Leeds, the Queen's Hotel,
that grandish pile of swank in City Square.
Too posh for me! he said (though he dressed well)
If you weren't wi' me now ah'd nivver dare!

I knew that he'd decided that he'd die
not by the way he lingered in the bar,
nor by that look he'd give with one good eye,
nor the firmer handshake and the gruff *ta-ra*,
but when we browsed the station bookstall sales
he picked up *Poems from the Yorkshire Dales* –

'ere tek this un wi' yer to New York
to remind yer 'ow us gaffers used to talk.
It's up your street in't it? ah'll buy yer that!

The broken lines go through me speeding South –

As t'Doctor stopped to oppen woodland yat . . .
and
wi' skill they putten wuds reet i' his mouth.

(Tony Harrison, 1987 *Selected Poems* Second edition.
Harmondsworth: Penguin)

This is one of a number of poems by the English poet Tony Harrison in which the narrator uses Standard English and his father's voice is represented in broad non-standard dialect, in this case the working-class dialect of Leeds in Yorkshire (in the north of England). Interestingly, Harrison does not just represent the dialect orthographically, but makes it, along with the Standard English parts, fit the rhythm and rhyme scheme of a 'sonnet' form. This both dignifies and seems to challenge the non-standard dialect in a way that would probably not have happened if the poet had chosen to use a genre traditionally more associated with dialect literature, such as the ballad. The two varieties of English seem to re-enact, in a sense, the social and familial tensions that the poem is exploring. The father's speech betrays his working-class background in that his regional dialect and accent are strongly marked (e.g. *'in't it'* for 'isn't it'; *'ah'd'* for 'I'd'; *'nivver'* for 'never'; *'this un'* for 'this one') and some of his lexical choices set him apart from more 'educated' or socio-economically privileged groups (e.g. *'ta-ra'* for 'goodbye' and *'gaffers'* for 'workers'[3]). The son-narrator's English, by contrast, betrays his educated and more independent status, as well as his feeling of 'distance' from his Yorkshire roots and upbringing. For him the hotel is no more than 'that grandish pile of swank', while it intimidates his father who says it is *'Too posh'* for him and that he would *'nivver dare'* to go there without his son (*'if you weren't wi' me now'*). The son is highly conscious of his father's speech, for example of the 'gruff' way he says *'ta-ra'*, yet is deeply moved when his father chooses to give him a book of dialect poetry before they part. Although the father feels overawed by his surroundings and conscious of his lack of education and his limited experience, he shows a proud defiance in hoping that the book will *'remind yer 'ow us gaffers used to talk'*. At the same time, however, this very gesture reveals how far he feels his son has detached himself or been detached through education and opportunity from his social and geographical roots. This is a poem that shows how fragile and unreliable the notion of class really is, since though he was born into a working-class family, the poet can no longer be said to be part of it. As Harrison journeys 'South' it is the 'broken lines' of connection between his father and himself, represented through their now sharply divergent social dialects, that haunt him. He reads of the doctor who *'stopped to oppen woodland yat'* and is reminded of his father's frail state of health, while the line *'wi' skill they putten wuds reet i' his mouth'* ('putting words right in his mouth') brings to mind contexts in which speakers of non-standard dialects are vulnerable to those speaking the more prestigious standard dialect. If we put words in someone's mouth we get them to say what they don't actually mean (for example, by getting them inadvertently to admit guilt or to incriminate themselves). The exploitation,

---

[3] *Gaffer*, thought to derive from *godfather*, has several meanings. *Workplace boss* or *supervisor* would come closest to the sense in which it is attributed to the poet's father here. The *gaffer* would not, however, be a white-collar worker or manager cut off from the ordinary workforce.

direct or indirect, of the dialectally disadvantaged and untrained by the dialectally privileged and adept is, perhaps, the true nature of the *skill* that Harrison reflects on here. Yet, ironically, it is only by learning to speak another, more educated dialect and by studying the language of other people that the poet has freed himself from the limitations of his social background.

1.5 Summary

In this chapter we have considered some of the fundamental dimensions of variation in English, paying particular attention to user-related variation. Individual language use varies in the sense that each of us has a constantly developing repertoire of speech styles. Our use of language also reflects the communities and social networks to which we belong, with particular language varieties or dialects playing an important role in constructing, maintaining and adapting identities. Finally, dialects and accents of English are constantly in flux, along with attitudes towards them, and so speakers of English do not necessarily use the same regional or social variety all their lives.

Activities

1. Make a list of the *social networks* which you feel you belong to, and consider in what way each influences the way you use your language. Which networks do you think are the 'strongest' (i.e. in having the greatest number of interconnecting links between their members)?
2. If you are bilingual or bidialectal, describe how membership of two (or more) *speech communities* influences your language use. For example, do you always use one of your languages or dialects in formal situations and the other in less formal contexts? Do you code-switch in certain situations and, if so, when and why?
3. Read the following opening verse from the poem 'Tommy' by Rudyard Kipling (1865–1936). The speaker is Tommy Atkins, a common soldier who has fought for his country. Note some of the features of his Cockney dialect, as represented in the poem, and try to work out how he feels about the way he was treated in the pub (public house).

> I went into a public-'ouse to get a pint o' beer,
> The publican 'e up an' sez, 'We serve no red-coats here.'
> The girls be'ind the bar they laughed an' giggled fit to die,
> I outs into the street again an' to myself sez I:
>   O it's Tommy this, an' Tommy that, an' 'Tommy, go away';
>   But it's 'Thank you, Mister Atkins,'when the band
>   begins to play –

The band begins to play, my boys, the band begins to play,
O it's 'Thank you, Mister Atkins,' when the band begins to play.

(Rudyard Kipling, 1892 *Barrack-Room Ballads and Other Verses*
Fourth edition. London: Methuen & Co.)

Further Reading

Holmes (2001), Spolsky (1998) and Wardhaugh (2002) are useful introductory texts to the study of language variation and sociolinguistics. They cover a wide range of topics, including speech communities, bilingualism, code-switching and variation in speech styles. See also Hughes and Trudgill (1996).

Chapter 2

Studying Varieties

2.1 Introduction

In this chapter we will look briefly at the kinds of linguistic analysis needed to study variation in English. Without at least the basic tools of such analysis, we can give little more than an impressionistic account of varieties. Of course, the goal is not to learn to describe formal features of language for their own sake. In studying varieties we need to bring together what we observe on the formal linguistic level with what we can discover or infer about context and other relevant factors, so as to come to a maximally informed description, judgement or interpretation, wherever the emphasis might lie. If you are studying varieties of English within a broader linguistics or English language studies course, I am sure you will need no persuading that acquiring the basic skills of description is important. However, even if, for you, language variation is just one dimension of more interdisciplinary studies, it is still worth acquiring at least some familiarity with the tools and methods of linguistics. Doing so will make you more perceptive in your observations about language variation and make it less likely that you will need to depend on generalisations or assumptions about particular varieties.

2.2 Sounds

This section will offer only a brief overview of the sounds of English, so readers with a particular interest in this area will need to consult more detailed accounts, such as Rogers (2000).

The first thing we need to do when looking at sounds is in fact not to *look* but to *listen*. This is difficult when you are reading, as you are now, but to make it easier we'll start by asking ourselves how many sounds there are in the following words: *cup*, *birth* and *cough*. In *cup* it is clear that there are three distinct sounds that match the spelling 'c-u-p', but in *birth* and *cough* the situation is not quite so straightforward. In *birth*, depending on whether we pronounce the 'r', we could say there are three sounds or four, but there are five letters in the word. Similarly, in *cough*, there are three sounds, but five letters. In some words, like *Leicester*, for instance, we might not be sure how many sounds there are, unless we happen to know how the name of this English city is pronounced. In fact it is pronounced 'lester', so again we either use five or six sounds here, depending on whether we pronounce the 'r'. Unlike some other languages that have a closer correspondence between spelling and sound, English is notorious for its lack of logic and predictability in this area. The reasons for this situation are of course historical, as we shall see in the next chapter. What matters here is to keep in mind the importance of distinguishing clearly between spelling and sound, in other words, between the orthography of English and its phonology.

Although people can often describe sounds by other means (e.g. by saying what they sound like, or rhyme with), the most accurate way of doing so is to learn to use the IPA or International Phonetic Alphabet. This provides symbols to represent all the sounds possible in languages, but of course for English we only need to use a selected set of them. Following are the IPA symbols for the consonants and vowels of the variety of British English pronunciation known as RP (discussed in Chapter 1), which I use in this book. Each symbol is followed by a word in which the particular sound occurs:

Consonants

Plosives (total closure of speech organs and sudden release of air):

/p/ p̲in /b/ b̲in /t/ t̲o /d/ d̲o /k/ c̲ot /g/ got

Fricatives (near closure and release with friction):

/f/ f̲ast /v/ v̲ast /θ/ t̲h̲in /ð/ t̲h̲en /s/ S̲ue /z/ z̲oo /ʃ/ s̲h̲oe /ʒ/ beig̲e̲
/h/ h̲ot

Affricates (total closure and release of air with friction):

/tʃ/ c̲h̲ore /dʒ/ jaw

Nasal sounds (air released through nasal passage):

/m/ m̲et /n/ n̲et /ŋ/ sin̲g̲

Approximants (speech organs approach each other, but without closure or audible friction):

/l/ l̲oad /r/ r̲oad /w/ w̲et /j/ y̲et

Vowels

Pure vowels:

/æ/ h<u>a</u>t /ɑ:/ f<u>a</u>ther /e/ w<u>e</u>t /ɪ/ s<u>i</u>t /i:/ s<u>ea</u>t /ɒ/ p<u>o</u>t /ɔ:/ c<u>augh</u>t /ʊ/ p<u>u</u>t /u:/ b<u>oo</u>t /ʌ/ b<u>u</u>t /ɜ:/ b<u>i</u>rd /ə/ <u>a</u>bout

<u>Note</u>: The symbol ː after a vowel indicates length.

Diphthongs (involving a glide from one vowel to another):

/eɪ/ s<u>ay</u> /aɪ/ t<u>ie</u> /ɔɪ/ b<u>oy</u> /aʊ/ n<u>ow</u> /əʊ/ kn<u>ow</u> /ɪə/ p<u>eer</u> /eə/ p<u>air</u> /ʊə/ d<u>oer</u>

These symbols represent *phonemes* or the smallest segments of sound that can distinguish two words. For example, in RP *leave* and *live* differ only in their respective vowels /iː/ and /ɪ/. Similarly, the words *pet* and *bet* are distinct from each other only because they have a different initial consonant. Pairs of words which differ only through one phoneme in this way are called *minimal pairs*. Of course, not every speaker of English will necessarily pronounce *leave* and *live* differently – in fact this happens to be a sound distinction which many learners of English across the world find difficult to produce, since it does not exist in their first language. In other words, speakers of English do not all have the same inventory or set of phonemes. Some accents pronounce the *r* after the vowel in words like *car* or *card* and are called *rhotic* accents; these distinguish between *law* and *lore*, whereas other accents may not. Most people from the north of England say *put* and *putt* the same way (using the vowel /ʊ/ for both words) whereas those in the south have a phonemic distinction here, using /ʊ/ for *put* and /ʌ/ for *putt*.

It is also important to note that there can be variation in the way a phoneme is pronounced, depending on where it occurs in a word or on the sounds next to it. In RP the phoneme /l/ has a 'clear' pronunciation when it occurs at the beginning of a word, but a 'dark' quality at the end of a word (compare *lip* and *pill*). These *actual* pronunciations or phonetic *realisations* of the /l/ phoneme are known as *allophones* or *allophonic variants*. We also have symbols or *diacritics* for these variant forms, as they are used in detailed or *narrow* transcriptions of speech. The 'dark' *l*, for instance, is written [ɫ]. Allophones are shown in square brackets, whereas phonemes are placed within slanting brackets. Another example of an allophonic variant in English is the dentalised variant of the /t/ phoneme, or [t̪], where the tongue tip is close to the upper teeth. This is normally the variant we find in the pronunciation of /t/ when it occurs before the dental fricative /θ/, as in the word *eighth*. Vowels, too, have allophones, such as the nasalised /ɪ/ in *sin*, where the nasal consonant /n/ affects the quality of the vowel sound immediately before it. This allophone is shown as [ĩ].

When people actually use the sounds of the language, they inevitably pronounce them in an individual way, that is with a particular voice quality that affects the actual sounds we hear. We all speak differently and indeed a person's voice is as individual as their face – although we may be good at putting on accents, few of us can actually sound exactly like another person. When someone *does* manage to sound very much like someone else (as do professional impersonators like Rory Bremner), they are able to manage it only after considerable scrutiny of their 'target' and continuous practice.

Vowels are sound units that typically occur as the 'nucleus' or main element of a syllable, and consonants typically occur at the beginning and/or end of a syllable, as can be seen in the case of the one-syllable word *cup*. When we articulate vowel sounds our vocal cords vibrate, producing *voicing*, and vowels are distinguished from one another through the movements of our tongue and lips (say the words *see, so* and *saw* in sequence and you will be aware of these changes, though the degree of difference will vary from one accent of English to another). Vowels can also be pure, as in *read* /riːd/, diphthongs, as in *road* /rəʊd/, where the first, stronger and louder vowel glides into the second without a break, or (more rarely) triphthongs, as in *royal* /rɔɪəl/, where the diphthong leads into a central vowel. Of the 12 pure vowels of English, some are also relatively long compared with others, as can be heard when we say *seat* /siːt/ and then *sit* /sɪt/, though the contrast is also one of quality as well as quantity, which is why there are different symbols for these sounds in the IPA. One vowel, the most common in RP, is the neutral vowel or *schwa* /ə/, which occurs in unstressed syllables, as in the second syllable of *brother* or *motor*. Schwa can be represented by a wide range of different spellings, as we see in the words *appoint, photograph, suppose* and *endless*.

Rhythmically, phonemes in words are grouped together to form *syllables*. In English a word of only one syllable can have just a single sound, like *awe* /ɔː/, or *ah* /ɑː/, but it can also have a sequence (*cluster*) of up to three consonants in front of the vowel and up to four consonants after it, as in *splashed* /splæʃt/ and *twelfths* /twelfθs/. In English, as in other languages, only certain combinations of consonants in a particular sequence are possible. We can have a sequence like *spr-* at the beginning of a syllable, but we can't alter it and have the sequence *rps-* instead. Usually, the minimal requirement for a syllable is the existence of a vowel (as in *awe*), and this is called the *nucleus* of the syllable. There are, however, words of one syllable with only a consonant sound, like *shh* or *mm*, and there is also a group of consonants that are usually syllabic in certain positions. For example, in the words *bottle* and *button*, the second syllable is formed from a syllabic allophone of the phonemes /l/ and /n/. To show this syllabic realisation, we use the diacritic of a small vertical line under the phonemic symbol, giving

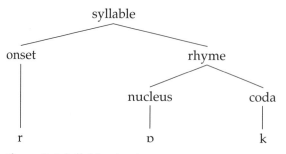

Figure 2.1 Syllable structure

us [bɒtl̩] and [bʌtn̩].Generally, though, most syllables have a vowel as the nucleus, with the possibility of one or more preceding consonants (called the *onset*) and one or more consonants following (the *coda*). If a syllable has a coda, the combination of the nucleus and coda is called the *rhyme*. So, if we take a monosyllabic word like *rock*, the structure of this syllable can be illustrated as in Figure 2.1.

Knowing how a syllable is structured in English can help us decide where the syllable boundaries come in words of more than one syllable, even though there might be some uncertainty about this and sometimes optional boundaries may be possible. In a word like *extreme* /ekstriːm/, for instance, we might feel the boundary between the two syllables could be placed either between /ek/ and /striːm/or between /eks/ and /triːm/, but we would be unlikely to place the boundary between /e/ and /kstriːm/, because in this case the second syllable would begin with an initial cluster of four consonants that does not occur in English words. From the phonological point of view, most of us would divide a word like *correspondence* /kɒrəspɒndəns/ into the syllables kɒ – rə – spɒn – dəns, because we know that this division conforms to common and easy-to-articulate sequences of sounds in English (note that we are concerned with units of sound here, and not units of meaning in words or etymology, which we will come on to in the next section). Of course, while there is likely to be a fair degree of agreement on the syllable boundaries in a word like *correspondence*, we need to remember that some words are pronounced differently in different varieties of English. In British RP *medicine* is generally pronounced /medsn̩/ so it has two syllables, whereas in American English it is usually pronounced /medəsən/ and has three syllables.

Because the rhythm of English is what is normally called **stress-timed**, certain syllables are naturally longer and more prominent than others within words. For example, in the three-syllable word *production* the main or primary stress is placed on the second syllable. To show this the IPA uses a small high-placed vertical line immediately before that syllable, so the word is transcribed /prəˈdʌkʃən/. In some words a secondary stress may also be indicated, this time by means of a small low-placed vertical line, as in *paranormal* /ˌpærəˈnɔːməl/. Just as some syllables are more prominent than others within words, so certain words are in turn more prominent than others within the 'sentences', or rather *tone units*, of speech. We will look more closely at the ways in which speech and writing differ as modes of communication later in this book. For now, I shall simply explain some of the key terms you will need to know to describe what happens to the sounds of English when they are combined.

Speaking at normal conversational speed, we often simplify our pronunciation in various ways. One way in which we do this is through *elision* (omitting sounds): *gonna* and *wannabe* are well-known forms of *going to* and *want to be* (in recent times *wannabe* has even become a noun with the derogatory meaning of someone who is trying to be like some other individual or group). Elision is also illustrated by the contracted forms used in the language, such as *it'll*, *should've*, *won't*, and so on. We can also elide or omit vowels, as in RP /pliːs/ for *police*, simplify consonant clusters in words and phrases like *next time*, saying /neks taɪm/ and link a word-final /r/ with a word-initial vowel sound, as in 'pour‿all the water‿away' (called 'linking *r*'). Another way of simplifying is through *assimilation*, when adjacent sounds influence each other in various ways. The second word in *Bridge Street* is likely to begin with the phoneme /ʃ/, under the influence of the affricate /dʒ/ at the end of the first word. In *ten books*, the 'n' is usually pronounced /m/ in anticipation of the bilabial (using both lips) sound to follow, while in the sequence *aren't sure* the phonemes /t/ and /ʃ/ coalesce to form a single new unit /ɑːntʃɔː/. In addition to these simplification processes there is a group of functional or grammatical words that in the native varieties of English have both a 'strong' and 'weak' form of pronunciation. If we say *Where's he from?*, the word *from* is given full stress /frɒm/, but when we say *He's from Oregon*, we use the weak form with its neutral vowel /frəm/. Further examples of the many words with both strong and weak forms include *and*, *that*, *his*, *of*, *to*, *some*, *there*, *have*, *were* and *must*.

In studying varieties of English you will often need to make observations about phonology. These can take a number of different forms, however. You might need to use your knowledge of IPA phonemes to describe the differences in the sound inventory of different varieties, as when transcribing a recording of someone speaking with a particular regional or social accent. You might be trying to see to what extent a particular speaker uses the sound system of a particular variety – as we saw in Chapter 1, individuals all have their own way of speaking and can modify their accents in various ways. Alternatively, you might need to deduce pronunciation from, say, an orthographic (spelling) representation of an accent. To illustrate some of the many contexts in which such representation of accents is used, here are just two examples. One was a newspaper headline, *In Toon with Disney*, and the other was written on a packet of 'Little Italy' vegetable lasagne: '*Eating vegetable lasagne always reminds me of my boyfriend Guiseppe*

[sic]. *He's chunky, full of goodness <u>anda</u> course he's got <u>greata</u> taste. After all he chose me!'* Of course ordinary orthography has its limitations in representing the pronunciation of varieties of English. For example, the glottal stop /ʔ/ rather than /t/ in a word like *letter* is a notably increasing feature of many varieties of British pronunciation, especially among younger speakers, but there is no consistently effective way of representing this feature in ordinary writing.

2.3 Words

If you were to point at random to the words of any common text like a newspaper article, you would probably come up with a set like the following: *the, political, fallout, in, anti-, GM crops.* Such an assortment reminds us that words come in all shapes and sizes and are often made up of smaller parts. To be able to analyse the structure of words is a helpful skill in studying the uses and effects of vocabulary, whether our focus is on a political speech, the conversation of members of a street gang, or a poem. This section will give a brief outline of the structure and formation of words. A more detailed introduction can be found in Jackson (1989).

The elements making up words are called *morphemes*, which are the smallest units of grammatical form. A word like *cat* consists of just one 'free' morpheme, because it can stand alone as a meaningful word. *Cats*, though, is made up of that free morpheme plus a 'bound' morpheme, the -*s* plural ending attached to it, which has no meaning on its own. Bound morphemes, as the name implies, have to be tied to another morpheme, whereas free morphemes can occur independently. A word like *went* represents two morphemes, despite its apparent simplicity, since it actually has two meaningful units: *go* + *past* (the word *went* is simply an irregular form which is not in itself divisible into two units). This becomes clearer if we compare *went* and, say, *wanted* (*want* + *ed*).

Bound morphemes can be either *inflectional* or *derivational*. In *wanted* the -*ed* is an inflectional morpheme, as it simply gives more information about the existing word *want* – it tells us that it is *want* in the past tense. However, the suffix -*y* in *cloudy* is a derivational morpheme, as it creates a new word from the noun *cloud*, fitting into a different grammatical slot, namely the adjectival slot, in the sentence. Thus, suffixes like -*able*, -*dom*, -*ful*, -*ism*, -*or*, -*ish*, -*ous*, -*hood*, -*ship*, -*ing* (forming a noun like *farming*) are all derivational. Inflectional suffixes include the third person singular -*s* ending, the possessive '*s* form, the present participle or -*ing* form (continuous) and the -*er* and -*est* forms of comparison. Now, to practise distinguishing free (F) morphemes from the derivational (D) and inflectional (I) bound morphemes, we will analyse the morphological structure of the following words:

reality real (F) + -ity (D)
historians history (F) + ian (D) + s (I)
closest close (F) + est (I)
represents re- (D) + present (F) + s (I)

Morphology is closely related to the next topic concerning words that we need to discuss here, namely word formation and vocabulary extension. In English the main processes involved are as follows:

Affixation: derivational morphemes or *affixes* are added to a word, either at the beginning as a *prefix*, like the *mis-* in *misunderstand*, or at the end as a *suffix*, like the *-ful* in *peaceful*.
Compounding: separate words are joined to create new words, as in *haircut*, *website* or *video-conferencing*.
Conversion: a word retains its form but changes its grammatical class to give a new word, as when *butter* is used as a verb.
Backformation: a new word is formed by removing rather than adding an element usually assumed to be an affix, as in *laze* from *lazy*, *enthuse* from *enthusiasm*, and *televise* from *television*.
Borrowing: using words from other languages, e.g. *yoghurt*, *perestroika* and *salsa*.
Clipping: when a word is created through shortening or reducing another word, as in *exam* (examination), *fax* (facsimile), *flu* (influenza), *lab* (laboratory).
Blending: two words are merged to form a new word, as in *brunch* from *breakfast* and *lunch*, or *smog* from *smoke* and *fog*.
Use of acronyms: a word is formed from the initial letters of a phrase, as in *laser* from *light amplification by stimulated emission of radiation*, or *Aids* from *acquired immune deficiency syndrome*.

In studying certain varieties of English we often need to describe the kinds of words associated with them. A good starting point is to consider whether the words used are morphologically simple or complex. A story written for young children to read, for example, usually has a simple morphological structure, but morphological structure in other kinds of communicative situation may be less predictable. A legal or medical expert responding to questions from the public on a radio phone-in programme has to strike a careful balance between the use of specialist and accessible words.

We may also need to explore word formation in some varieties, such as advertising or poetry. Many ads create new words not only to name new products but also to describe their effects and qualities. An ad for the Nissan Micra car makes explicit reference to the word-formation process of blending through which it has created new words summing up the qualities of the new model: *simpology* ('simple' and 'technology'); *modtro* ('modern' and 'retro', itself a clipping from 'retrograde') and *spafe* ('spontaneous' and 'safe'). Having given us this quick lesson in word formation, the ad finally teases us with the question 'Do you speak Micra?', suggesting that this is a 'language' we ought to continue learning by purchasing the car.

2.4 Phrases and sentences

Words belong to word classes like nouns, verbs and adjectives. In a simple sentence like *Kate looks tired*, *Kate* is a noun (a proper noun, as it is a name), *looks* is a verb and *tired* is an adjective. More often than not, however, in real as opposed to illustrative language, the positions of noun and verb and so on in a sentence are made up of more than just one element per grammatical class. For example, instead of *Kate*, we could begin the sentence with *The new lecturer*, so this time we would have, instead of a single noun, a **noun phrase** formed of the definite article (*the*) plus an adjective (*new*) plus a noun (*lecturer*) as the subject of the sentence. Also, instead of a single verb we could have the combination of verbs *is looking*, which we call a **verb phrase**, and instead of a simple adjective like *tired*, we could have *ready to drop*, giving us a more complex **adjective phrase**. Therefore, it makes more sense to think of words in sentences as the elements of potential phrases rather than as totally independent items.

A phrase may have one or more other phrases within it, which is called **embedding**. For example, if we change *the new lecturer* to *the new lecturer in our department* the noun phrase now has the prepositional phrase *in our department* embedded within it. This can be illustrated by means of what we call a *tree diagram* (in fact an upturned tree – see Figure 2.2), which has the advantage of allowing us to show through nodes and branches how one element can be part of another. Another way of showing this embedding is by means of bracketed notation; this has the advantage of taking up less space on the page and being easier to create: [NP [NP the new lecturer] [PP in our department]].

Sentences can be divided into **major sentences**, which can be broken down into regular patterns like subject-verb-object-adverbial, and **minor sentences**,

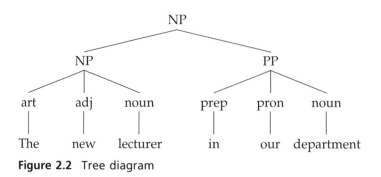

Figure 2.2 Tree diagram

which do not have this regularity in construction and cannot be changed in the range of ways that major sentences can (e.g. with specific elements substituted by others). Examples of minor sentences include *How do you do?*, *Here today, gone tomorrow, No smoking*. Each of these has a formulaic or proverbial quality, which means that public notices usually say *No smoking* and not, for example, *Don't smoke*.

If a sentence consists of only one clause, like *She writes books*, it is a **simple sentence**. If it contains more than one clause, it is a **multiple sentence** and either *compound* or *complex*. In a compound sentence, the clauses are joined by **coordination**, usually through the use of a *coordinating conjunction* like *and*, *or*, or *but*. The clauses of a compound sentence could also stand alone as an independent clause, as in *He did the course and he passed the exam*. Often we find that in a sentence of this kind an element in the second (or third etc.) clause is left out through **ellipsis**, so that we have *He did the course and passed the exam*. However, we still say that both clauses can stand independently, since the missing element is obviously understood. Complex sentences are linked through **subordination**. Here, a *subordinate clause* that follows a *subordinating conjunction* like *when, because* or *although* is dependent on another clause, the *main clause*, and cannot stand on its own as an independent sentence, as we see in *Although I like films, I don't go to the cinema very often*.

This has been no more than a brief account of phrase and sentence structure in English. Readers may need to refer to more detailed introductions, such as Burton-Roberts (1997).

2.5 Texts

We now come to the level of language beyond the sentence, namely the level of text or discourse. The terms 'text' and 'discourse' can sometimes be used interchangeably, but most applied linguists today would distinguish between them. In calling a multi-sentence piece of language a 'text', we focus more on its formal linguistic patterning, but in calling it 'discourse' we focus more on its social context and function, including sometimes its role in representing and constructing ideologies. Because the focus in this chapter is on formal structure and patterns, the word 'text' is used in preference to 'discourse'. Later on, however, when we look at aspects of English in context, the latter term will be a lot more important and useful to us.

A text can be defined as a piece of spoken or written language which we recognise as having a complete or autonomous communicative function. Even very short messages, like a sign saying *Parking Prohibited*, are texts in this sense. Normally, a text is a longer sequence of sentences that relate to each other in ways that produce **coherence**. Not all sequences of sentences form texts – they have to be coherent sequences, making some sort of sense together. Of course, our familiarity with the context in which a particular stretch of language is used and our ability to infer meanings that may not be explicitly stated play an important part in our ability to recognise the coherence of a text. For the moment, however, we are concerned with the internal cohesive features of a text, not these additional or 'external' factors, which will be explored later.

Here is a description of a new device for use in supermarkets. It provides a simple illustration of some of the ways in which the language of a text can be cohesive:

> An electronic scanner which can read the entire contents of a supermarket trolley at a glance has just been developed. Virtually eradicating supermarket queues, the *Superscanner* could revolutionise the way people shop. It would do so, firstly, by removing the bottleneck which causes most customer frustration and, secondly, reducing the number of checkout staff.

Obviously, most of the vocabulary of this text concerns supermarket shopping, so we find *lexical cohesion* through all the words to do with this activity: 'supermarket', 'trolley', 'shop', 'customer'. Other words are related by similarity of meaning, such as 'queue' and 'bottleneck'. There is also *grammatical cohesion* in the text: the determiner 'the' in 'the *Superscanner*' refers back to 'An electronic scanner' (this is called *anaphoric reference*), and the pronoun 'it' in 'it would have a double benefit' also looks back to 'the *Superscanner*'. The text also uses grammatical *substitution* in 'it would do so' (i.e. with 'do so' substituting 'revolutionise the way people shop') as well as *ellipsis* or omitted elements: there is no *by* before 'reducing', because it is understood from the previous structure 'by removing'. Finally, connecting adverbials occur in the text, with 'firstly' and 'secondly' performing a linking function.

As I intimated above, the coherence of a text, even a simple one like this, is not solely a matter of internal links and ties of the sort we have just looked at. In addition to 'processing' the text with the help of such connections, we also draw on our own general knowledge about supermarket shopping, about what a scanner is, and make inferences, where necessary, about what we are reading. For example, we realise that the second and third sentences of the extract depend on the inferred connection *If the scanner were introduced*.

In looking at texts, we also consider whether the information in them is presented and arranged in a logical sort of way, one that we recognise as consistent with the kind of text, or *genre*, that we are dealing with. Certain types of text, like news reports, have fairly predictable patterns of organisation, taking us, for example, from a newsworthy piece of information to its possible consequences or effects. Other texts, like some poems, may seem to destabilise the notion of normal coherence, sometimes leaving us baffled and unable to see connections between particular words or sentences. Take, for example, this enigmatic poem by Emily Dickinson:

> We do not play on graves
> Because there isn't room;
> Besides, it isn't even,
> It slants and people come
>
> And put a flower on it,
> And hang their faces so,
> We're fearing that their
>   hearts will drop
> And crush our pretty play.
>
> And so we move as far
> As enemies away
> Just looking round to see
>   how far
> It is occasionally.

(Ralph W. Franklin, ed. 1999 *The Poems of Emily Dickinson:*
Reading Edition Cambridge, Mass.: The Belknap Press of
Harvard University Press)

Crystal (1995) discusses this poem as an example of a text which 'bends' the conventional uses of pronoun reference. There is an illogical grammatical link in line 3, where we would expect the pronoun *they* rather than *it* (because of the plural *graves* in line 1). This seems to force us to adjust *graves* to *grave* as we read the second verse. By the third and final verse, *It* has taken on a complex range of meanings: as a reference to a particular grave and, we guess, to death itself, but also perhaps as a reference to the earlier phrase *as far/As enemies away* (i.e. a reference to how far that might be). The more we read and think about a text like this, the more we have to activate our brains to search for less obvious links and associative meanings. Thus, coherence does not *have to* depend on logical internal links and familiar patterns of organisation – it also has a lot to do with how we interpret the language we read or hear.

2.6 Summary

In this chapter I have outlined some of the basic skills we need to describe the linguistic forms of English, from sounds to texts. In looking at the different varieties covered in this book we will draw from time to time on some of the descriptive labels introduced here, so they should become a lot more familiar as we go along. In the meantime, the next chapter will turn to the beginnings of Modern English and discuss some of the landmarks on its way to international status.

Activities

1. Transcribe each of the following words. Note that if you are transcribing a rhotic accent of English you will have an additional consonant in (e) and (g):

   a. speech
   b. plays
   c. guide
   d. knee
   e. afford
   f. autumn
   g. rehearsed

2. Write out the following transcription (based on standard southern British English) in ordinary spelling and add suitable punctuation. It summarises an episode of a British TV series of the 1990s about a retired woman in Yorkshire who becomes a private detective. The transcription opens with the name of the woman who played the starring role (Patricia Routledge):

   / pə'trɪʃə 'rautlɪdʒ slɪps ɪntə hə 'sensəbl̩ ʃuːz fər ə'nʌðə raund əv 'æmətə 'sluːθɪŋ | ə laːdʒ 'ɔːdɪəns ɪz ˌgærən'tiːd | tə'naɪts sə'naːrɪəu kən'sɜːnz 'pɔɪzm̩ pen letəz/

   In the transcription above identify the following:

   a. three words containing a diphthong
   b. a word with the consonant /vowel sequence of cvcvccvc
   c. three grammatical words in their weak forms
   d. an example of assimilation or any other simplification feature.

3. Divide each of the following words into their component morphemes, labelling each morpheme (F) for free, (I) for inflectional or (D) for derivational:

   Example: differences = differ (F) + ence (D) + s (I)

   a. finds
   b. melted
   c. combinations
   d. footnote
   e. helplessness
   f. typical
   g. weakened

4. Identify the word-formation or vocabulary extension processes exemplified by the italicised words in the following passage from a novel:

> In a *whirlwind* few days Ed Dunkel married Galatea, with Dean rushing
> around to get the necessary papers, and a few days before Christmas they
> rolled out of San Francisco . . . headed for *LA* and the *snowless* southern road.
> In LA they picked up a sailor in a travel *bureau* and took him along for
> fifteen dollars' worth of *gas* . . . All along the way Galatea . . . kept complain-
> ing that she was tired and wanted to sleep in a *motel*.
>
> (Jack Kerouac, 2004 *On the Road* London: Penguin)

5. Identify some of the cohesive links in the following text:

> This course introduces several of the main issues, aesthetic, historical, polit-
> ical and social, that are involved when discussing Beethoven's music. It
> aims to evaluate how his music reflects its time, as well as to identify the
> changing development of its style and assess its historical significance and
> influence. The course is in five main sections, each concentrating on a par-
> ticular theme. It assumes that you are familiar with the rudiments of music,
> have a reasonable understanding of traditional harmony and can follow a
> score.
>
> (Adapted from *Open Opportunities 1991/92* Milton Keynes:
> Open University)

Further Reading

For concise accounts of the description of English, see Finch (1998) and
Aitchison (1995). Yule (1996) provides a good introduction to the study of
language, covering description and language varieties. Also useful are the
relevant sections in O'Grady, Dobrovolski and Katamba (1997). One of the
best large-scale reference books on the grammar of current English is Biber
et al (1999). For an introduction to English syntax see Burton-Roberts (1997).
For the phonology of English see Rogers (2000) or Roach (2000). See also
Jackson (1989) on morphology and semantics.

Chapter 3

The March of Modern English

3.1 Introduction

No study of varieties of English in the modern era can afford to ignore the key events and influences in the development of the language. In this chapter we will look at the roots of 'modern' English, at the standardisation processes that have accompanied the language and its evolution into a 'global' language and international lingua franca.

Modern English is most simply defined as a third stage in the history of the language, beginning around 1450 (the first two being the Old English and Middle English stages). However, this three-stage chronological model of the language is generally refined by linguists, with Modern English itself seen as divisible into distinct phases, normally called 'Early Modern English' (1450–1700) and 'Modern English' (1700 to the present day). Some linguists argue for a further stage in the language, beginning around 1945 and called 'Late Modern English' or 'World English', reflecting the globalisation of English as an international lingua franca.

3.2 Early Modern English

During the Early Modern English phase a number of highly significant and liberating changes took place in English society that were to have a profound effect on the way the language was to be used and regarded. During the 16th and 17th centuries the concept of the autonomous nation state became a reality in Europe. In the growing market economy there was a breaking away in England from the authority of the Catholic Church through the period called the Reformation.[1] There were rapid developments in Europe in the areas of medicine, science, the arts and theology, all of which had an impact on the English language, and the beginnings of colonial exploitation of Africa, Asia and the Americas brought a further dimension of change. However, if there was one event that was to have a more profound

---

[1] This religious movement in Europe set out to reform (hence its name) Roman Catholic doctrines and practices.

effect on English than any other, it was probably the establishment in London of William Caxton's printing press in 1476 and the subsequent publication of books and translations in English (notably the English translation of the Bible in the mid-16th century). The new print medium demanded that a decision should be made as to which regional variety of English should be used in books to be read throughout the country, and Caxton chose the variety he knew best – that of London. In fact, a preference for the London standard was already apparent in most literary writings by the mid-15th century, as well as in official records, notably documents written by clerks of Chancery. While Caxton followed this trend, however, his work showed much inconsistency and it took a further century for printed texts to attain any kind of uniformity.

The selection of a dialect was the first step in the development of a standard English that was to be codified as time went on through the work of lexicographers and grammarians. Indeed, *selection* and *codification* are two of the four processes that linguists have identified as essential to standardisation. The other two are *elaboration* (through which the dialect is made more suitable in various ways for its role as a standard) and *implementation* (through which it is used in an increasingly wide range of contexts and text types). These processes may, but need not, happen at the same time and will depend on the extent to which the linguistic community is conscious of norms of communication or is what linguists call a *focused* community.[2]

While the works of classical authors were made more accessible through translation during the Early Modern period, not everyone agreed about the suitability of English for scholarship and literature. This is hard for us to believe today, but we need to bear in mind that up to this point scholars had used Latin and Greek as the language of learning and had not thought of English as being sufficiently refined or 'eloquent'. As a result, they now felt that something needed to be done to English to make it more suitable for the expression, for example through literature, of a more confident sense of national and cultural identity. So the fashion began in earnest for introducing new words and restoring obsolete words, for using words from English dialects such as *algate* ('always') or *sicker* ('certainly'), for adopting words from Latin or Greek or borrowing them from other languages. Words like *alienate* (from Latin), *passport* (from French), *lottery* (from Italian), *canoe* (through Spanish, but originally from Carib *canaoua*) and *landscape* (from Dutch) are all loan words that came into English during the Early Modern period. The English lexicon increased dramatically between 1500 and 1700, when it is thought that about 30,000 words were added to it. William

---

[2] Le Page and Tabouret-Keller (1985) propose the phenomenon of 'focusing' and argue that a linguistic community may be focused if, for example, it has a sense of common cause or recognises the usage of a leader or influential group as prestigious.

Shakespeare (1564–1616) is the writer whose work casts most light on what was happening to the English language at the time, whether we think of pronunciation, vocabulary and word formation, syntax or the social use of the language. Crystal (1995) includes the following in his list of some of the words first recorded in Shakespeare that are still in use today: *countless, dwindle, laughable, premeditated* and *submerged*. The words found in Shakespeare that have *not* survived in Modern English are frequently his neologisms (coinages) from Latin, such as *abruption, exsufflicate, tortive* and *vastidity*. During Shakespeare's lifetime there was much debate on the pros and cons of using Latinisms. On the one hand, Latin had been the established language of learning and authority; on the other, purists were opposed to what they called 'inkhorn terms' and advocated the use of plainer words of Germanic origin.[3] The growth of Protestant ideals following the Reformation encouraged the defence of intellectual freedom and egalitarian ideas, the expansion of science (not yet opposed to religion), and the championing of English as a language capable of both expressing the new ideas and bringing *all* English people together as a nation.

Now that we have surveyed some of the main influences on the state of the language in the Early Modern period, I will explore a short 17th century text that illustrates a number of the things we have discussed so far. When John Milton's English and Latin poems appeared in 1645, the publisher, Humphrey Moseley, added the following short preface to the reader (shown here in modern typeface but retaining the original spelling and punctuation):

> It is not any private respect of gain, Gentle Reader, for the slightest Pamphlet is nowadayes more vendible then the Works of learnedest men; but it is the love I have to our own Language that hath made me diligent to collect, and set forth such Peeces both in Prose and Vers, as may renew the wonted honour and esteem of our English tongue: and it's the worth of these both English and Latin Poems, not the flourish of any prefixed encomions that can invite thee to buy them, though these are not without the highest Commendations and Applause of the learnedst Academicks, both domestick and forrein: And amongst those of our own Countrey, the unparallel'd attestation of that renowned Provost of Eaton, Sir Henry Wootton: I know not thy palat how it relishes such dainties, nor how harmonious thy soul is; perhaps more trivial Airs may please thee better. But howsoever thy opinion is spent upon these, that incouragement I have already received from the most ingenious men in their clear and courteous entertainment of Mr Wallers late choice Peeces, hath once more made me

[3] The term was first used by Thomas Wilson in his *Art of Rhetorique* (1553) to denote an ostentatious or obscure word. Among the examples he gave were 'revolting' and 'magnifical dexteritie'. An inkhorn was a container for ink, and so appropriately brought to mind the usage of scholars. Wilson wrote: 'Among all other lessons this should first be learned, that wee never affect any straunge ynkehorne termes, but to speake as is commonly received: neither seeking to be over fine nor yet living over-carelesse, using our speeche as most men doe, and ordering our wittes as the fewest have done. Some seeke so far for outlandish English, that they forget altogether their mothers language.'

adventure into the World, presenting it with these ever-green, and not to be blasted Laurels. The Authors more peculiar excellency in these studies, was too well known to conceal his Papers, or to keep me from attempting to sollicit them from him. Let the event guide itself which way it will, I shall deserve of the age, by bringing into the Light as true a Birth, as the Muses have brought forth since our famous Spencer wrote; whose Poems in these English ones are as rarely imitated, as sweetly excell'd. Reader if thou art Eagle-eied to censure their worth, I am not fearful to expose them to thy exactest perusal.

Thine to command

HUMPH. MOSELEY

(John Milton, 1968 *English Poems – Comus 1645* A Scolar Press Facsimile: Menston)

There are several things to note about this text. First of all, in terms of what it actually tells the educated reader of the day, what comes across very clearly is a confidence in the validity of English as a literary language. Moseley writes that he loves his own language and that his publication 'may renew the wonted honour and esteem of our English tongue' and ends by saying that he is not afraid to subject the poems he has chosen to publish to the most demanding or 'exactest perusal' of critics. Such remarks suggest that, although English was still sharing a platform with Latin at this time, it was becoming the main focus of publishing interest. Another point to note from the preface is that publishing in English was also beginning to cater more for popular tastes; indeed, Moseley indicates he has difficulty competing against the producers of pamphlets and does not expect any financial gain from publishing Milton's poems – the tone he uses here is not in fact very far removed from that of the typical small poetry publisher of our own day!

There are also several interesting points to note about the language of the extract. Moseley uses the second person pronoun forms *thou/thee/thy* in addressing the reader. Around the time of the publication of Milton's poems the use of *thou* was less common in standard usage and not as respectful as *you*, the form that people of lower rank would normally use to those above them. In Shakespeare's day *you* had also been the form used by children to parents and by members of the upper classes when talking to each other. Perhaps Moseley's choice of *thou* reflects a sense of superiority (in literary taste and discernment) over the reader, a characteristic arguably consistent with the description of Moseley by Dobranski (1999) as a 'high-minded and self-appointed guardian of fine literature' who tended to use his introductory epistles in part to reflect his own status and discrimination as a bookseller. However, it is equally possible that the use of *thou* could suggest closeness to his reader socially (c.f. *Gentle Reader*).

In the original manuscript the printing conventions of the text appear to be fairly regularised and not too far from modern style, though two variants of 's' are used (i.e. the modern orthographic symbol and the straightened lower-case variant known as 'long s' which was used in script and printing until the 18th century). We can see that the symbols 'u' and 'v' are distinguished, as in *invite* and *famous*, though the distinction between *u* as a vowel and *v* as a consonant was not stabilised in print until the 17th century. As for punctuation, the text has many features familiar to us. We find capitals used at the beginning of sentences and full stops at the end, though there is clearly a stylistic preference for the alternative use of the colon and semi-colon, particularly in the first half of the passage. With regard to the apostrophe, we find the modern use for contraction in *it's the worth of these both English and Latin Poems*. However, the presence or absence of the apostrophe appears to indicate variability in pronunciation of 'ed' endings in the adjectives *unparallel'd* and *renowned*, and the apostrophe is absent from the possessive structure in, for instance, *Mr Wallers late choice Peeces*. The comma is more frequently used than in English today: it comes between subject and verb in *The Authors more peculiar excellency in these studies, was too well-known* and interrupts the comparative in *as rarely imitated, as sweetly excell'd*.

The text makes prolific use of capitalisation of nouns, following the fashion of the day: capitals are used not only for proper nouns and titles like *Henry Wootton* and *Provost of Eaton*, but also selected abstract nouns like *Commendations* and concrete ones like *Papers*. Actually, this trend was to continue till the later 18th century, when new rules were introduced restricting the type of nouns thought appropriate for capitalisation.

The spelling used in the text is again largely familiar to the modern reader. When the preface appeared, the use of final 'e' was not yet consistent, as shown by *Vers* and *palat*, but doubling of letters was popular, as in *Peeces*, *forrein* and *sollicit*. On the whole, though, we recognise the spellings used as very close to those of today and as having the same unpredictability between spelling and sound, as in *highest, courteous, honour, conceal* and *attempting*.

The overall style of the preface is elegant and heavily influenced by Latinate vocabulary and constructions. Some words are no longer in use today, such as *vendible* ('saleable') and *encomions* (formal praises), which would no doubt have been labelled 'inkhorn terms' by the advocates of plainer lexis. Many others are now archaic or have undergone shifts in meaning, among them *wonted, dainties, peculiar* and *entertainment*.

The grammar has some typical Early Modern English features. I have already commented on the use of *thou*, but we also find here the so-called *-eth*-morpheme in *the love I have to our own Language hath made me diligent to collect. . . .* During the 16th century *hath* was increasingly replaced by *has* in the standard spoken language, but *hath* continued to appear in formal writing and can be found in some poetic works even in the 20th century. Barber (1993:185) tells us that *hath*, along with the *-eth* forms *doth* and *saith*, held on longer than others and was often used in the 17th century, so it is not surprising to find the form in our text. In *I know not thy palat how it* *relishes such dainties* there are two grammatical points of interest, the first being *I know not*, which in Modern English would be *I do not/don't know*. The *do* auxiliary was acquiring its Modern English functions during the Early Modern period, but it could still appear as a 'dummy' or merely stylistic variant, as in *they did build a tower*, where we would say *they built a tower*. In more formal or stylised contexts it might also be omitted in negative and interrogative forms, and Barber (1993:191) notes that expressions such as *I know not, Say you so?* and *What think you?* were still common in the late 17th century. The second point of interest is the word order of *thy palat how it relishes* (rather than 'how thy palat relishes'), an example of 'left dislocation' generally avoided in formal writing today.

Overall, the sentence structure is quite complex, making use of embedding and dependent clauses, as in *But howsoever thy opinion is spent upon these, that incouragement I have already received . . . late choice Peeces, hath once more . . . World, presenting it with these . . . Laurels*. This, along with the formal tone of the vocabulary and a tendency towards nominal structures such as *the highest Commendations and Applause* and *the unparallel'd attestation*, make our text a good example of the way English was written by a professional, cultured man of the 17th century.

As we move on to the 18th century and the end of the Early Modern period we reach the age in which English was subject to the most obsessive standardising forces in its history. Spelling was now more strictly regularised in printed books and, because it was based on earlier pronunciation, preserved many of the idiosyncrasies that we know today, for example in the retention of letters representing sounds that are no longer pronounced, such as the *k* in *knee* or the *t* in *castle*. Many people had by now become quite reactionary in their attitudes to changes in the language (they used words like 'barbarous' and 'unruly' to describe what they saw as the chaotic speed and randomness of these changes). So it seemed to several writers and commentators of the time that the answer might lie in the establishment of some kind of body or academy to protect the most acceptable standards of usage. However, when Jonathan Swift, following Dryden and Defoe before him, produced 'A Proposal for Correcting, Improving and Ascertaining the English Tongue' in 1712 and advocated the setting up of an academy, there was no widespread support for the idea. Instead, people argued that the job of taking control of the language and making it more consistent and logical should be left to the producers of dictionaries, grammar books, spelling and punctuation guides, and this was what in fact took place.

In his authoritative *Dictionary* of 1755 Samuel Johnson included definitions of about 40,000 words and drew on the best contemporary speech around London and quotations from highly selective literary sources, such as the writings of Sir Philip Sidney (1554–1586), to illustrate their uses. Though Johnson had initially planned to 'preserve' the best English he could find, the preface to the *Dictionary* itself describes his function in a less prescriptivist tone as to 'register the language', not to 'form' it. However, in general, as Barrell (1983) has noted, Johnson was essentially conservative in his defence of the usage of polite society and believed that a national standard for the language was as important as the unity of the nation.

The task of imposing order on the grammar of English was enthusiastically taken up by, among others, Bishop Robert Lowth in his *Short Introduction to English Grammar* (1762). Lowth and other grammarians judged usage according to such criteria as 'gracefulness', 'solemnity' and 'elevation' of style, and so took no account of what might be natural in speech or appropriate to informal contexts. Among some of the things they condemned as improprieties are *who is this for, it is me* and *I had rather not*. A later influential grammarian was Lindley Murray, whose *English Grammar* (1794) also helped to establish the view towards the end of the 18th century that grammar books should tell people both how to use the language and how *not* to use it, rather than simply describe the ways in which English was actually being used at the time.

The first half of the 19th century saw the publication of many dictionaries both in Britain and the United States. Noah Webster (1758–1843) produced his highly influential *An American Dictionary of the English Language*, a work that aimed to supplant Johnson in its greater coverage of words connected to American life and institutions and its advocacy of more logical spellings, such as the American spellings of *honor, color, traveler*, and so on. This dictionary, though attacked in Britain for what was seen as its disrespect to Johnson's work, made Webster a household name in the States. Throughout the 19th century a more mobile population responding to the needs of the new industrial society and becoming more interested in social nuances was fuelling a growing demand for works about varieties of English that differed from the standard language. Thus dictionaries and glossaries were also published about the vocabulary of a number of regional dialects. The importance of the novel as an entertainment also increased the opportunity to experience different varieties of English through the regional, social and personal variations in the speech of different characters, notably in the works of Charles Dickens. Earlier the Romantic movement had also drawn attention to the way ordinary people spoke, for example in the poetry of William Wordsworth (1770–1850) and in his much-quoted *Preface* to the second edition of *Lyrical Ballads* (1800). Here, he rejected the artificial diction of the 18th century neo-classicists whom he accused of ignoring the language actually used by ordinary people. This did not mean that Wordsworth himself wholly succeeded in bringing ordinary language into his own poetry (after all, poetry is not in fact 'ordinary' language anyway), but it did reflect a movement away from the view that good writing was necessarily in the elegant, refined style associated with privileged members of society.

In the 19th century, however, there were other major influences on the development of English and, in particular, of Standard English. Compulsory state education was introduced in Britain in 1870, so greater numbers of people now encountered Standard English and were encouraged to use it in speech and in writing. However, it was the spread of both British and American English to many other parts of the world that now took centre stage in the story of the language. Many British colonies were established (e.g. in Sierra Leone in 1808, Singapore in 1819, Nigeria in 1861) and Australia became a British dependency in 1829. In 1835 British rulers of India officially endorsed English as a language of education for Indians and in 1863 The Cambridge Overseas Examinations were established. In 1819 the US purchased Florida from Spain, and in 1821 American settlers arrived in the then-Mexican territory of Texas, which became a state of the US in 1845. Obviously, these are just a sample of the events that contributed to the rapid spread and increasing importance of the English language across the world.

3.3 The growth of international English

The 20th century saw the continuing expansion of English and its eventual transformation into a global language. In 1900 English was almost exclusively the language of the British Empire and the US, but after 1950 it was to become the main medium of communication for thousands of organisations worldwide, for broadcasting, the press, advertising, the film and music industries, the academic community, international transport and communications. When the *Encarta World English Dictionary* was published in 1999, its introduction stated that approximately 375 million people spoke English as their first language and that more than that number spoke it as their second language. Below are some of the main areas of 20th century life in which English played a leading role. For a more detailed account see Crystal (1997:78–112).

The film and music worlds

Since the 1920s English has dominated the film industry, and by the end of the 20th century the US controlled most of the film market worldwide. Today English language films and TV programmes are shown in many countries in which English is taught as a foreign language (e.g. Denmark), undubbed and sometimes even without subtitles. The popular music scene in both Britain and the US spread rapidly to the rest of the world through a recording industry dominated by the English language. An indication of the assumed importance of English to success in the pop world is seen in the fact that the Swedish group ABBA chose to record all their major hits in English.

Broadcasting

Radio is another important area of influence, particularly English-language broadcasting produced specifically for listeners in other countries. Both the Voice of America (since 1942) and the BBC World Service (since 1932, when it was called the Empire Service) have broadcast English-language programmes to audiences of millions, with the American English services developing the most far-reaching network of stations throughout the world.

Travel and safety

International travel is another domain in which the English language has come to play a central role. Most package tourism uses English at least as an auxiliary language, and when we enter the tourist information websites of major cities all over the world, the language we usually find is English.

English has, since the early years of the International Civil Aviation Organization, founded in 1944, been the official lingua franca of air travel. English is also the lingua franca of the sea, giving rise to the artificially standardised variety known as *Seaspeak*. More recently bodies involved in the cross-border handling of emergencies have supported the development of *Emergencyspeak*, intended to codify this kind of communication between the UK and its European neighbours.

English Language Teaching (ELT)

In 1990 Bill Bryson wrote: 'The teaching of English, according to *The Economist*, is worth £6 billion a year globally. It is estimated to be Britain's sixth largest source of invisible earnings, worth some £500 million a year' (1990:177). Towards the end of the decade Crystal (1997) reported that the British Council 'has estimated that, by the year 2000, there will be over 1,000 million people learning English'. The use of English has become universal in many academic disciplines, with the majority of scientific papers now being published in English. It is also the medium of instruction in higher education in an increasing number of countries. In the Netherlands, for instance, courses in fields such as law and medicine are often taught through the medium of English. Also, as Crystal (1997:103) has pointed out, with greater international student mobility, universities and colleges throughout the world can argue that they need a lingua franca to cater more successfully for 'mixed-language audiences'. These trends also have an effect on the number of international students choosing to enrol on English courses before embarking on their chosen degree studies. No longer is the advanced English language course needed only by those aiming to take a degree in the language, to be English language professionals such as translators and interpreters, or to teach English themselves in schools and colleges. It is, arguably, needed just as much by prospective scientists, doctors, nurses, lawyers, businesspeople and many other specialists.

English is now introduced to more and more children in non-English speaking countries at primary school level (and even earlier in some areas). Therefore, before they meet it formally in the educational context, children may already have encountered English through computer games, the media and people around them. Interestingly, in these contexts, the words they encounter may well be the product of code-mixing between English and their first language. A German child, for example, may be familiar not only with *sweatshirt* but also *Cordhose* (corduroy trousers) and a host of other mixed compounds to be found, for instance, in catalogues or on clothing labels.

The fact that more and more school pupils of all ages encounter English in informal contexts outside the foreign language classroom is an inevitable challenge to native-speaker models in use within the teaching curriculum and examination system. Teachers may find it virtually impossible to insist on, say, a British English standard pronunciation in class when students are exposed to more flexible and inventive uses of English within youth subcultures outside.[4]

Borrowings from English

The phenomenal growth in the international community of users of English has led indirectly to ever-increasing borrowings from English within other languages. Many of these are, however, innovative in their form and specific in meaning to the linguistic and cultural contexts in which they are used. In German, for example, the English word *matchmaker* is used to mean someone who organises sports fixtures rather than marriages, and a *Crashkurs* (crash course) is what politicians are said to be on when headed for a serious confrontation with the opposition, not when they are following an intensive course in some subject of interest to them. Germans talk on their *Handy*, whereas Brits talk on their 'mobile' and use 'handy' as an adjective meaning 'convenient' or 'useful'. When the German Post Office produced a leaflet in the late 1990s (see Figure 3.1) to advertise self-assembly packages called *LuckyPäcks* (without a space between the two words and with an umlaut above the 'a' to represent German pronunciation, but retaining the English plural form), they were sending out a message of confidence in their exploitation of English, happily breaking English spelling rules to interest and entertain their home target market. Note the use of the borrowed words *Service*, *Limit* and *Set*, each of which could have been replaced by German words:

---

[4] See Preisler (1999) for an interesting discussion of tensions between the official promotion of English in Denmark and its use within the popular domains of English-oriented youth subcultures.

Jetzt Bis 31. Mai: Frühling beim Paket–Service
LuckyPäcks
packen!

Die Päckchen
ohne 2-Kilo-Limit:
Einmalig mit
praktischem PackSet L
inklusive Porto
DM **7,90**

Deutsche Post

Figure 3.1 Borrowing from English: Deutsche Post

3.4   Attitudes to English usage

Although English is a vibrant and global lingua franca, it is surprising how often people try to argue that it is becoming degenerate and that others are failing, wilfully or otherwise, to use it 'correctly'. We need to tread warily when we broach the subject of 'correctness', however, as views about changes in English usage can be very entrenched indeed. Very often those who write letters of complaint about current English to the newspapers are not in fact complaining about the language at all, but about other things, such as social or cultural changes that alarm them. Complaints about the spread of so-called 'Estuary English' in the 1990s tended to centre on the assumption that it went along with laziness or sloppiness. Letters I collected on the subject at the time included the following comments: *it is not an accent . . . just lazy speaking that grates on the ear and is an extremely bad example to our children*, and *The spread of Estuary English can only be described as horrifying. We are plagued with idiots on radio and television who speak English like the dregs of humanity . . .* This second commentator went on to make a more general complaint about apparent misuse of the language, homing in on one of the most popular targets of the self-appointed language regulator, namely the split infinitive: . . . *we hear at least two split infinitives a day. I wrote to the BBC on this matter a year ago, only to be informed by some minion working for the corporation that the English language is changing. I am not aware of this and neither are any other educated people in this country. The only change is the increasingly slovenly use of speech.* Without realising it, however, this writer had revealed the true source of his intolerance: he was unaware that living languages are always changing and that natural linguistic change of this kind is not something we need to worry about.

Many of the attitudes people still have towards the use of English have their roots in the prescriptive approaches favoured by many commentators and grammarians of the 18th and 19th centuries. The prohibition on the use of double negatives, for instance, can be traced back to the book on English grammar written by Bishop Robert Lowth (see above) who argued that 'two negatives in English destroy one another, or are equivalent to an affirmative'. In fact, although this may sound logical enough, it falls down when we consider that language offers us more than simple two-way distinctions. To say something is *not untrue* does not mean we think it is therefore unambiguously true – we probably have some reservations about it. And in everyday speech people use all kinds of negatives in sequence without usually obscuring their intended meanings. If a colleague asks me *Will you be going to the staff development seminar?* and I reply *Not this week, I won't*, I am not likely to be misunderstood. Of course, certain kinds of double negatives come in for particular criticism, but this is for social, not linguistic, reasons. Teachers in schools discourage the use of structures like *I didn't go nowhere* in discursive writing (and probably also in formal speech in class) because, although they are widely used in the community, they are not part of the grammar of current Standard English and are therefore stigmatised in educational contexts.

People who worry about changes in pronunciation or the use of words and grammar of English tend, if they aren't making accusations of vulgarity or sloppiness, to adopt what Aitchison (1997) calls the 'crumbling castle' view, seeing themselves as defenders of a fine structure that shouldn't be allowed to fall apart. Alternatively, they correctly see change as something that comes about through social contact, but wrongly interpret this as justifying a need to fight against possible 'infection' of the language by 'diseased' forms and usages. Such complaints show that Standard English is often assumed to be a superior dialect to all others, although this is not true, since the differences between dialects are mainly social rather than linguistic. The grammar of one dialect is not automatically in itself superior to that of another, but people often think this must be the case if one of them has greater social prestige than the other. We may not think this matters very much when it is in the interests of society to promote good educational standards and effective communication, but real damage can be done when people make subjective judgements about others purely on the basis of their accent, for example denying them equal treatment or opportunity in employment.

Young people have always tried to distinguish themselves linguistically from their elders. However, as society becomes less deferential (especially in the British context) it is arguable that children and young adults are now more likely to adopt what older generations might consider to be stigmatised features of grammar and pronunciation. The vocabulary choices and accents of young people are also to some extent influenced by those of media personalities such as pop and sports idols.

As more people from a wider range of social backgrounds enter higher education, a wider range of accents can also be heard among professional groups like academics, lawyers and doctors. If you compare recordings of British English news broadcasts made in the first half of the 20th century with recordings today, you will find that, overall, the articulation of English sounds has become less tense and clipped. Although the use of the glottal stop is a traditional Cockney feature in words like *butter*, pronounced /bʌʔə/ and has been generally stigmatised, the substitution of a glottal stop for /t/ at the end of words like *foot* or *street* is now spreading rapidly, and even newsreaders whose speech is considered exemplary in terms of clarity now use it quite frequently.

When new English dictionaries are published there is generally a great deal of public and academic interest in how points of disputed usage are explained and dealt with. Those who fear erosion of standards look eagerly for concessions made to slang and informality, while others look for evidence of greater democratisation of the language through entries on variant forms and international usage. In recent years several new dictionaries have begun to address both usage and the internationalism of English in more thorough ways. One of these, *The New Oxford Dictionary of English*, published in 1998, sets about reappraising many of the traditional debates about good usage, drawing evidence from the British National Corpus (a corpus of 100 million words of British English from the early 1990s – about 90% written and 10% spoken) and other sources of authentic and up-to-date usage. In their Introduction the editors recognise that questions of usage are often affected by important changes in social attitudes (as in the case of politically sensitive words such as the use of *man* to mean *humankind*, or potentially offensive uses of words like *native* or *race*). They also accept that change in the language cannot be blocked, as shown by the fact that 'the prescriptions of pundits in the past have had remarkably little practical effect on the way the language is actually used' (p. xv). They define 'good usage' as 'usage that gets the writer's message across, not usage that conforms to some arbitrary rules that fly in the face of historical fact or current evidence' (p. xv). Significantly, they also add that their 'underlying approach has been to get away from the traditional, parochial notion that "correct"

English is spoken only in England and more particularly only in Oxford or London', an aim which they claim to have fulfilled with the help of a 'network of consultants in all parts of the English-speaking world' (p. xvi). Looking at usage from an international point of view, they tell us that the 'picture that emerges is one of complex interactions among an overlapping set of regional standards' (p. xvi).

The dictionary that has done most to reflect the globalisation of English, however, is undoubtedly the *Encarta World English Dictionary*, referred to earlier and published in 1999. Its central aim is to meet the needs of a diverse worldwide audience and it claims to be the first to be available in both print and electronic form.[5] The hard data on which the definitions of the *Encarta* dictionary are based derive from the Corpus of World English, compiled by experts specifically for this dictionary and containing over 50 million words reflecting world varieties of the language. Like *The New Oxford Dictionary of English*, the *Encarta World English Dictionary* provides special entries on points of usage and adopts a non-prescriptive approach to many issues of concern to the purists. Both dictionaries rightly recognise that it is more important nowadays to advise speakers on the possible implications of words (especially those likely to give offence to some people or in some places and contexts) than to take a pedantic line on issues such as the use of *hopefully* as a sentence adverb or the use of a noun like *data* (the Latin plural of *datum)* with a singular English verb. These dictionaries are helping to explain to contemporary users of the language that certain types of worries about English are more justifiable than others, and that attempting to stop the language from changing is, as even the rather conservative Samuel Johnson understood in the preface to his great dictionary, a futile endeavour. If we ask ourselves what it is that makes us feel strongly about the way other people use English, we may find that the source is completely irrational.

3.5 Summary

In this chapter we have considered both the sources of Modern English and the development of the complex notion of a Standard English. The rapid evolution of the language into the global lingua franca that it is today raises a number of questions about the processes through which one language may thrive while others are doomed to extinction. While the ever-increasing use of English in the world eases international communication and perhaps strengthens understanding between nations and cultures, it also threatens the survival of other languages and their communities. These issues certainly

[5] The *Oxford Advanced Learners' Dictionary* and the *Longman Dictionary of Contemporary English* were also available in both electronic and printed form a few years earlier.

cannot be ignored when we study geographical varieties of English, the focus of the next chapter.

Activities

1. Read the following extract from a letter written by Lady Brilliana Harley to her son Edward Harley. Lady Harley wrote a series of letters between 1638 and 1643. They were almost all written in her own hand and, because most of them were written to her son, often had an informal style. This was the period of the English Civil War, and when she wrote the letter shown here, Lady Harley was in fear of being besieged by Royalist forces in her home at Brompton Castle near the town of Ludlow, England.

   Some questions to think about:

   Find some examples in the extract of words in use today that you feel probably had different meanings in 17th century England. Also list any words and grammatical structures that you think are no longer in common use. You could consult reference books such as the *Oxford English Dictionary* to check your hunches.

   > For my deare sonne Mr. Edward Harley.
   >
   > My deare Ned – I longe to see you, but would not haue you come downe, for I cannot thinke this cuntry very safe; by the papers I haue sent to your father, you will knowe the temper of it. I hope your father will giue me full derections how I may beest haue my howes gareded, if need be; if he will giue the derections, I hope, I shall foolow it.[. . .]
   >   Had I not had this ocation to send to your father, yet I had sent this boy vp to Loundoun; he is such a rogeisch boy that I dare not keepe him in my howes. . . . Giue him what you thinke fitte, and I desire he may not come downe any more, but that he may be perswaded to goo to seae, or some other imployment. . . . I pray God blles you and presarue you in safety, and the Lord in mercy giue you a comfortabell meeting with
   >   Your most affectinat mother, BRILLIANA HARLEY
   >   *Letters of the Lady Brilliana Harley*, ed. Thomas Taylor Lewis
   >   (London Camden Society 58, 1854)

2. Read the following extract from Thomas Hardy's novel *Tess of the D'Urbervilles* (first published as a novel in 1891). It describes a conversation between Tess and her mother. Tess has just paid her first visit to the Stoke d'Urberville family, to whom her parents, John and Joan Durbeyfield, believe they are distant relations. Being poor, they hope to establish a connection through Tess with this family, but in fact the Stoke d'Urbervilles have simply adopted an ancient name and Tess is eventually seduced and ruined by their son Alec. Tess has already become

uneasy about Alec's attentions to her. Consider how the representation of their speech in this passage contributes to our impressions of both Tess and her mother:

> When she entered the house she perceived in a moment from her mother's triumphant manner that something had occurred in the interim.
>
> 'Oh yes; I know all about it! I told 'ee it would be all right, and now 'tis proved!'
>
> 'Since I've been away? What has?' said Tess rather wearily.
>
> Her mother surveyed the girl up and down with arch approval, and went on banteringly: 'So you've brought 'em round!'
>
> 'How do you know, mother?'
>
> 'I've had a letter.'
>
> Tess then remembered that there would have been just time for this.
>
> 'They say – Mrs d'Urberville says – that she wants you to look after a little poultry-farm which is her hobby. But this is only her artful way of getting you there without raising your hopes. She's going to own 'ee as kin – that's the meaning o't.'
>
> 'But I didn't see her.'
>
> 'You zid somebody, I suppose?'
>
> 'I saw her son.'
>
> 'And did he acknowledge 'ee?'
>
> 'Well – he called me Coz.'
>
> 'An' I knew it! Jacky – he called her Coz!' cried Joan to her husband. 'Well, he spoke to his mother, of course, and she do want 'ee there.'
>
> 'But I don't know that I am apt at managing fowls,' said the dubious Tess.
>
> 'Then I don't know who is apt. You've be'n born in the business, and brought up in it. They that be born in a business always know more about it than any 'prentice. Besides, that's only just a show of something for you to do, that you midn't feel dependent.'
>
> 'I don't altogether think I ought to go,' said Tess thoughtfully. 'Who wrote the letter? Will you let me look at it?'
>
> 'Mrs d'Urberville wrote it. Here it is.'
>
> The letter was in the third person, and briefly informed Mrs Durbeyfield that her daughter's services would be useful to that lady in the management of her poultry-farm, that a comfortable room would be provided for her if she could come, and that the emolument would be on a liberal scale if they liked her.
>
> 'Oh – that's all!' said Tess.
>
> 'You couldn't expect her to throw her arms round 'ee, an' to kiss and to coll 'ee all at once.'
>
> Tess looked out of the window.
>
> 'I would rather stay here with father and you,' she said, nervously reflecting. 'But why?'
>
> 'I'd rather not tell you why, mother; indeed, I don't quite know why.'
>
> (Thomas Hardy, 2003 *Tess of the D'Urbervilles* London: Penguin)

3. Here is an idea for a possible project on diachronic change in English. Using a library or the Internet, try to find two texts in English, preferably from a single domain (e.g. newspaper editorials) but written about 50

years apart. Compare them to see how aspects of English usage have changed in the course of the period separating them.

Further Reading

Graddol, Leith and Swann (1996) contains a well-illustrated account of the historical landmarks in the language. Barber (1993) is a concise study of English from its beginnings through to its establishment as a world language. See Freeborn (1992) and Burnley (2000) for analyses of a range of illustrative texts from Old to Modern English. See also Bauer (1994) and, for attitudes to English, Crystal (1984), and Bauer and Trudgill (1998). See Bex and Watts (1999) and Milroy and Milroy (1991) for further discussion of Standard English.

Chapter 4

English from a Global Perspective

4.1 Introduction

When Australian tennis star Lleyton Hewitt was interviewed immediately after winning the 2002 Men's Singles final at the Wimbledon championships, he referred colloquially to the trophy he was holding as a *ripper*. No doubt a large number of the spectators who had just witnessed his victory didn't know exactly what the word meant, but guessed from the context and Hewitt's delight that it could only have been something very positive. In Australian English *ripper* means an excellent or outstanding thing or person, while, in stark contrast, in British English the word usually means a murderer who kills and mutilates with a knife, as in *Jack the Ripper*. Thanks to global media coverage, the mental lexicon of millions of non-Australian English-users must have undergone a simultaneous readjustment at that moment. Of course, I don't mean to suggest by this that speakers of British English, for example, are not familiar with at least some Australian slang. In a world of international travel, global media and communications, few of us are cocooned from the sounds and vocabulary of the major international varieties of English. So I need to be cautious in my assumptions about those Wimbledon spectators. Those who are regular viewers of the Australian soap *Neighbours* probably had no difficulty at all understanding Hewitt's use of *ripper*.

A similar need for caution should extend to the ways in which we label or model international varieties of English. In this chapter I will adopt, for convenience, the now well-established model suggested by Braj Kachru (1989), which describes the spread of global English in terms of three concentric circles:

Inner Circle

Territories in which a standard English is the first or main language (e.g. British Isles, US and Canada, Australia and New Zealand). Other languages are also used in these areas, but English is the dominant language. Crystal (1997:53) reports that 'The USA has nearly 70 per cent of all English mother-tongue speakers in the world (excluding creole varieties).'

Outer Circle

Territories in Asia and Africa to which English was first transported in colonial contexts and where it has since existed alongside very different local languages. Many people use English as a second language within these multilingual contexts and the language also has an institutional and administrative importance. In these settings new Englishes with their own distinctive formal and discoursal characteristics have developed and have often been promoted through postcolonial literatures, popular culture, etc.

Expanding Circle

Territories in which English has become or is becoming the most important foreign language. Though these countries do not have historical colonial links with the Inner Circle, they increasingly support the learning of English as an international language. These territories include China, Japan, Brazil, Israel, Poland and Russia. Naturally, to have a picture of the total numbers of people who speak English as a foreign language, we would also need to take into account those countries in which English has been taught as the main foreign language for a longer time, such as Germany, France and Mexico. The number of people who have acquired some competence in English in the Expanding Circle has already overtaken the number of people that speak it in the Outer Circle.

The three circles model attempts to represent the spread of English without encouraging over-simplified categorisation of users according to the native versus non-native yardstick. However, the model needs to be used flexibly. While it encourages us to equate the Inner, Outer and Expanding Circles with the use of English as a first, second and foreign language respectively, these are often less than accurate labels. Not everyone in an Inner Circle territory speaks English as a first language; not everyone in the Outer Circle speaks it as a second language and those who use English routinely in the course of their work in Expanding Circle countries might not consider themselves to be speakers of English as a 'foreign' language at all.

It is important to remember that the Inner Circle does not have limitless power over the development of English in the Outer and Expanding Circles. Indeed, Graddol (1997) and Crystal (1997) have both emphasised that English is moving into an era where speakers of English as a first language will lose influence as most communication will be among those using it as a second or foreign language. Today the Inner Circle's influence still emanates outwards, yet the exact nature and extent of this influence are sometimes difficult to determine. Attitudes towards the status of British or American English in postcolonial and multilingual cultures can be complex and unpredictable (English may of course be less favoured in some contexts than an indigenous language). Even where English is an official and preferred language, the development of new Englishes (a process sometimes referred to as *x-isation*, e.g. Indianisation, Africanisation) has enabled speakers and writers in the Outer Circle to challenge the traditional supremacy of Inner Circle Standard Englishes. Similarly, recent research suggests that some countries in the Expanding Circle have also begun to develop distinctive ways of using English, with the result that the language has an increasingly important functional range in these countries and is also a marker of identity in some contexts.[1] As the 'ownership' of English becomes pluralistic and can no longer be debated solely in relation to the Inner Circle, so the attitudes of those whose first or main language is English, as well as those who have traditionally looked to the Inner Circle for their norms of usage, are likely to be challenged in new ways.

Bearing this complexity in mind, in this chapter we will look at English in an Inner, Outer and Expanding Circle territory respectively. My choice of American English for the Inner Circle needs little justification, since this variety is now more influential in global terms than any other Inner Circle variety, although British English continues to have a significant impact on ELT in many parts of the world. This can be seen with regard to Indian English, for example, which I have chosen to represent the Outer Circle. Japanese English has been chosen as an illustration of an Expanding Circle variety, not least because the combined forces of English teaching and globalisation in Japan have provoked a timely debate on the cultural and educational impact of Anglicisation in countries in which it is the dominant foreign language learnt.

4.2 Inner Circle: American English

American English is, strictly speaking, spoken in Canada and parts of the Caribbean as well as in the US, but since most of its speakers live in the US and routinely call themselves Americans, it is not surprising that it is US English that most people associate with the term 'American English'. I will follow this convention here, also using 'Standard American English' or 'Network English' to refer more specifically to the most prestigious variety. In the context of this chapter, my central interest is in American English

---

[1] A colloquium held at the BAAL (British Association for Applied Linguistics) 35th Annual Meeting at Cardiff University 12–14 September 2002 looked at the varied functions that English performs for German and Finnish users in the domains of work, education, media and social life. Ongoing research reported by Elizabeth Erling and Alan Walton of the Freie Universität Berlin and Sirpa Leppänen, Arja Piirainen-Marsh and Tarja Nikula of the University of Jyväskylä suggested that the growing role that English now has in these countries requires a new way of looking at Kachru's three circles model and a new debate on the implications for English teaching in Europe. For information about BAAL see their website at http://www.baal.org.uk.

as the most influential 'Inner Circle' variety, rather than in the history and development of the language within the US itself. I will therefore restrict myself here to a necessarily selective survey of some of the main American English dialects and their characteristics, and to attitudes to American English within the US that speakers of English in other parts of the world are likely to be aware of. In restricting myself to a general overview based mainly on regional differences, I do not wish to ignore the importance of social and ethnic variation in American English. Indeed, two of its most widely debated and controversial varieties, African American Vernacular English (AAVE) and Hispanic English, will be discussed in their own right in the next chapter.

4.2.1 Regional dialects

The dialect boundaries in the US have been significantly affected by the high degree of social and geographical mobility that has characterised American life through successive waves of settlement and immigration. In general, it can be said that American English dialects are more homogeneous than British English dialects. Dialect differences are most distinctive in the east, the area of original primary settlement, while there has been more dialect merging in the west, as settlers and immigrants from different areas and speech communities have come together and influenced each other. The traditional belief, before major dialect studies were undertaken, was that American English could be divided into two main dialects, Yankee (Northern) and Southern. Hans Kurath, working on the *Linguistic Atlas of New England* in the 1930s and 1940s, proposed a three-way split between Northern, Midland (subdivided into North and South Midland) and Southern dialects, a division which was followed for about 40 years. However, subsequent research into lexical variants by Craig Carver (1987) tended to support a basic North/South split, though with a 'Lower North' and an 'Upper South' subdivision. Similarly, findings by Labov in an investigation of phonological variation and ongoing telephone survey (TELSUR) have supported, in the main, Carver's basic dialect boundaries.[2]

A few examples of differences between some regional dialects and General American or Network English are in order here, though these are necessarily selective. In the characteristic speech of Eastern New England, for instance, rhotic /r/ is lost after vowels, as in *far* or *hard*, while it is retained

---

[2] In fact, according to Fennell (2001: 229) Labov's 'findings to date suggest that currently the United States can be divided into three dialect areas, the North, Midland and South (along similar boundaries to those Carver described as North, Lower North, Upper South, and South) but with a further area which he regards as the West...'. She adds, however, that 'the major distinction still remains, that is that there is still validity in the North/South divide, which looms so large in the history and the national consciousness of the United States'.

in all positions in General American. A rounded vowel has been retained in Eastern New England in words like *top* and *dot*, whereas General American uses an unrounded vowel. Another Eastern New England characteristic is the use of /ɑ/ in words like *bath*, *grass*, *last*, etc., where General American uses /a/. In these respects the New England accent shows some similarities with British RP.

Currently vowels appear to be undergoing noticeable change in several areas of the United States. For example, in large cities such as Chicago and Detroit, the place of articulation of the long low vowels is moving forwards and upwards, making the /ɒ/ of *coffee* sound more like the /ɑ/ of *father*, and that of the short vowels is moving downwards and backwards, making words like *mock* or *hock* sound like *mack* or *hack*. Other examples of the change include words like *sample*, which sounds like *simple*, and *steady*, which sounds like *study*. These changes can be heard particularly clearly in the speech of younger people and are part of the process usually termed the Northern Cities Shift or Northern Cities Vowel Rotation.

Characteristics of the Southern dialect areas include the well-known 'Southern drawl', which is produced largely through a combination of slower enunciation and diphthongisation of stressed vowels, so that a word like *class* is pronounced like [klæɪs] or [klæjəs]. Final consonant clusters may also be weakened in words like *kind*, *fast* and *slept*. No distinction occurs in much of the South between words like *pen* and *pin*, the mid vowel /e/ being raised to a high front vowel before nasals. As in New England, *r*-lessness is a characteristic of Southern speech, though the post-Second World War trend towards pronouncing postvocalic *r*, much associated with Labov's sociolinguistic studies in New York (Labov 1966), has also influenced the South, in particular the speech of younger people.

Grammatical features found in Southern American English include the use of a special pronoun for the second person plural, *you-all*. This is usually written *y'all* and pronounced [jɑl] and has a genitive form, *you-all's* or *y'all's*, as in *We saw y'all's car in the parking lot*. Other nonstandard features associated with Southern grammar include the use of *a*-prefixing, as in *She's a-workin'*, the use of *done* with an adverbial function meaning 'already', as in *he done got fired* (restricted to working-class speech), and the combination of two modal verbs, as in *He might could bring the truck*. One rather unusual non-standard feature found in informal usage in a number of American regional dialects is the use of *anymore* in positive sentences to mean 'nowadays', as in this example from the *Encarta World English Dictionary*: *We always use a taxi anymore*.

Both New England and the South also have distinctive dialect words. Many of these are connected with regional foods, such as *corn chowder* (a soup) and *cruller* (doughnut) in New England, *grits* (boiled cornmeal) and *gumbo* (a soup or stew) in the South. Some of the terms for foods are loan words from Native American languages, reflecting the fact that the early settlers were introduced by Native Americans to a wide range of new foods and ways of cooking.[3]

While such regional differences enrich the vocabulary of American English, we shouldn't overstress their importance. Much of the lexicon of American English reflects a non-rooted spirit and the mobility associated with both the American past and contemporary way of life. The arrival of train travel in the 19th century brought a large number of new words and expressions into the language, as can be seen in this second extract from the novel *On the Road*:

> 'During the depression,' said the cowboy to me, 'I used to *hop freights* at least once a month. In those days you'd see hundreds of men riding a *flatcar* or in a *boxer*, and they weren't just *bums*, they were all kinds of men out of work and going from one place to another and some of them just wandering. It was like that all over the West. *Brakemen* never bothered you in those days. I don't know about today. Nebraska I *ain't* got no use for. Why in the middle nineteen thirties this place wasn't nothing but a big dustcloud as far as the eye could see. . . .' [my italics]
>
> (Jack Kerouac, 2004 *On the Road* London: Penguin)

To *hop freights* means to jump on board a train without paying. A *flatcar* is a railway freight wagon without a roof or sides, while a *boxer* is a fully enclosed wagon with sliding doors. The term *bum* (derived from the German 'Bummler') is, like *hobo*, associated with rail travel and means a vagrant. *Brakemen* refers to those operating the brakes on the train. While not a lexical feature, the contraction *ain't* is particularly frequent (though often stigmatised) in informal American speech of the kind represented here by Kerouac.

4.2.2 Attitudes

Lippi-Green (1997) discusses several studies that have claimed that Northerners tend to have little understanding of the diversity of the South, to evaluate the *Southern Trough* or *Deep South* negatively as a place to live in, and to be condescending towards Southern speech in general. Southerners' attitudes are, of course, as important as those of people in the North or elsewhere in the country in continually recreating and reinforcing assumed regional differences. Southerners will often represent themselves as more down-to-earth and natural than Northerners, more committed to family values and more spiritual. In the North, however, this representation can sometimes reinforce assumptions that Southern culture is small-town, narrow-minded and given to superstition, thus perpetuating the sense of a divide. Such attitudes towards cultural differences cannot be separated from

---

[3] See Bryson (1994) for an interesting account of the history of food and cooking in America after the arrival of the original settlers.

attitudes towards dialect. Believing they could be disadvantaged by their pronunciation, some Southerners have attended accent-reduction classes, but resistance to the dominance of mainstream US English is generally more common. As in other Inner Circle territories, speakers of stigmatised dialects in the US may react to their stigmatisation by emphasising their separate identity and speech more strongly, thus making their variety of English a symbol of solidarity and giving it *covert prestige*. This does not of course prevent such varieties from being a source of entertainment for those who do not use them, as can be seen in the following orthographic representation, purportedly from a tourist guidebook, of the local speech of Georgia:

Jawjuh wurds

... from The Essential Guide to the Southern states of America ... Top Ten Local Expressions:

Bard (verb). Past tense of the infinitive 'to borrow'. Usage: 'My brother bard my pickup truck'.

Jawjuh (noun). A highly flammable state just north of Florida. Usage: 'My brother from Jawjuh bard my pickup truck.'

Bahs (noun). A supervisor. Usage: 'if you don't stop reading these Southern words and git back to work, your bahs is gonna far you!'   [*boss ... fire*]

Retard (verb). To stop working. Usage: 'My granpaw retard at age 65.'
                                                                [*grandpa ... retired*]

Farn (adjective). Not local. Usage: 'I cudnt unnerstand a wurd he sed ... must be from some farn country.'   [*foreign*]

Did (adjective). Not alive. Usage: 'He's did, Jim.'   [*dead*]

Bob war (noun). A sharp, twisted cable. Usage: 'Boy, stay away from that bob war fence.'   [*barbed wire*]

View (contraction): verb and pronoun, used as a question. Usage: 'I ain't never seen New York City ... view?'   [*have you*]

Gummit (noun). An often-closed bureaucratic institution. Usage: 'Not another gummit shutdown!'   [*government*]
                                                                (My italics.)

(Desmond Christy, copyright Guardian Newspapers Limited 1996)

Studies of 'folk' or perceptual dialectology in the US have shown that both the South and the Northeast, particularly New York City and New Jersey, are popularly associated with 'incorrect' English. Such research has highlighted the importance of affective or emotional dimensions in the labels that respondents to surveys have used to describe the varieties of US English. For example, as Hartley and Preston (1999) have shown, references to a negatively perceived language variety tend to go beyond observations on the language itself and to be connected to stereotypes and caricatures of the people who use it (e.g. 'cowboys', 'rednecks', 'hillbillies') and their supposed manner or behaviour (e.g. 'rude', 'slow', 'aristocratic').

4.3 Outer Circle: South Asian English

After the US and UK the Indian subcontinent has the largest number of users of English. The distinctive varieties of English in this region, which comprises India, Bangladesh, Pakistan, Sri Lanka, Nepal and Bhutan, are now usually called collectively 'South Asian English', although the term 'Indian English' traditionally referred to the subcontinent (as the former 'undivided India'). Technically, this term is now limited to English usage in the Republic of India.

Beginning in the early 1600s, the British East India Company, granted a charter by Queen Elizabeth I, set up trading stations and settlements in Madras, Calcutta and later Bombay. With the decline in European rivalry and the power of the Moguls, the Company gradually extended its power and influence and took administrative control in some areas. By the time the Company was dissolved and its powers taken over by the Crown in 1858, English was on its way to being established as the language of administration in India. English became more influential as the period of British sovereignty (called the *Raj*) continued, its role being further strengthened by the foundation of the universities of Bombay, Calcutta and Madras in the mid-19th century. To the British colonial rulers, English was seen as a means of ensuring effective government through the creation of a subculture of Indians schooled in the language and able to act as skilled interpreters.[4]

The status of English became less certain as Indian nationalism grew in the first half of the 20th century, leading to the country's independence in 1947. However, the prediction of Jawaharlal Nehru (1889–1964), the first Prime Minister of independent India, that English would not survive another generation was not fulfilled. Given the complexity of the linguistic situation in India, with its large number of indigenous and local languages, English was eventually regarded as the most logical choice as a unifying lingua franca, despite its colonial associations. In the 1960s the 'three-language formula' was agreed, stipulating that all citizens should learn a national, a regional and a local language. Since then English has had several legislated roles: as an associated official language alongside Hindi as the official one, as a national language alongside Hindi, Bengali and Tamil, as the state language of Manipur, Meghalaya, Nagaland and Tripura, and as the official language of eight Union territories.

The following extract from a classic novel set at the time of partition in 1947, reflects the important role of English in education as well as ambivalent

---

[4] This is shown vividly in the proposal by the imperialist historian Thomas Macaulay in 1835 for the creation of 'a class who may be interpreters between us and the millions whom we govern – a class of persons, Indians in blood and colour, but English in taste, in opinion, in morals and in intellect'.

attitudes towards it at a time of growing religious tension and conflicting loyalties:

'What will you do with English?' Iqbal asked. 'The sahibs have left. You should learn your own language.'

Jugga did not seem pleased with the suggestion. For him, education meant knowing English. Clerks and letter writers who wrote Urdu or Gurmukhi were literate, but not educated.

'I can learn from anyone. Bhai* Meet Singh has promised to teach me Gurmukhi, but I never seem to get started. Babuji, how many classes have you read up to? You must have passed the tenth?'

Tenth was the school-leaving examination.

'Yes, I have passed the tenth. Actually I have passed sixteen.'

'Sixteen! Wah, wah! I have never met anyone who had done that. In our village only Ram Lal had done four. Now he is dead, the only one who can read anything is Meet Singh. In the neighbouring villages they haven't even got a bhai. Our Inspector Sahib has only read up to seven and the deputy Sahib to ten. Sixteen! You must have lots of brain.'

Iqbal felt embarrassed at the effusive compliments.

'Can you read or write anything' he asked.

'I? No. My uncle's son taught me a little verse he learned at school. It is half English and half Hindustani:

Pigeon – *kabootur, oodan* – fly
Look – *dekho, usman* – sky

Do you know this?'

'No. Didn't he teach you the alphabet?'

'The A B C? He did not know it himself. He knew as much as I do:

A B C where have you been?
Edward's dead, I went to mourn.

You must know this one?'

'No, I don't know this either.'

'Well, you tell me something in English.'

Iqbal obliged. He taught Jugga how to say 'good morning' and 'goodnight'. When Jugga wanted to know the English for some of the vital functions of life, Iqbal became impatient. Then the five new prisoners were brought into the neighbouring cell. Jugga's jovial mood vanished as fast as it had come.

Bhai is a title of respect for a distinguished Sikh – Meet Singh is a priest.
(Kushwant Singh, 1988 *Train to Pakistan* New Delhi: Ravi Dayal)

It might be somewhat ironic that this fictional exchange between characters with very little English is itself narrated in English by an Indian writer who is using that language to represent the complexity of Indian identities. Yet it is as distinct from the English of England as is Welsh, Irish, African or Caribbean literature in English. What all these 'postcolonial' or 'new' English literatures have in common is that they have appropriated English confidently for their own ends and given it a new and unmistakable distinctiveness.

4.3.1 Features of South Asian English

The local languages of the region, such as Bengali in Bangladesh and Sinhala in Sri Lanka, have an influence on English usage in terms of pronunciation, grammar and vocabulary. However, there is still a degree of uniformity in South Asian English, the result of both similarities among Indian languages and of British administrative, commercial and educational influence, particularly the English-medium schools based on a British model of the language. The phonological characteristics of the variety include its rhoticity (/r/ is pronounced in words like *port*, *floor* and *worker*), its tendency to use fairly evenly stressed vowels in words like *open*, and the 'singsong' quality of its intonation. Common grammatical features include the use of *wh-* questions without inversion of word order (as in *Why he is going there?*) and the use of *only* for emphasis in sentence-final position (*They are coming once a week only*, instead of *They come only once a week*). This last example also shows a variation of aspect associated with spoken Asian English in its use of the progressive *are coming* rather than the simple aspect *come* for habitual meaning. Other typical features are the undifferentiated use of the tag *isn't it*, as in *She is with them now, isn't it?* and the adverbial use of *there* instead of the introductory or 'dummy' *There is/are*, for example, *Fruit is there, plates are there*.

Local words and expressions are commonly used in South Asian English, as in *dhobi-wallah* ('laundryman'), the numerical terms *lakh* (one hundred thousand) and *crore* (ten million), or *bandh* (local strike) and *lathi* (police truncheon). Occasional Indianisms are used in English-language newspaper reports, such as the following from the *Calcutta Telegraph*, quoted in McCrum, Cran and MacNeil (1987:324):

> Frequent *dacoities* and looting of fish from *bheris* in the Sonarpur area has created a serious law and order problem. Tension prevails in the entire area which has 60 bheris. *Dacoits* armed with pipe-guns, swords and sticks strike before the villagers can retaliate.
>
> [*dacoities /dacoits:* attacks/bandits; *bheris:* fish farms]

In this way South Asian English is indigenised lexically and immediately recognisable as a distinctive variety. The process began in the colonial period, as British administrators adopted an ever-increasing number of local words and phrases, many of which, like *brahmin, bungalow, jute, purdah* and *chutney*, are still well known as borrowings into English today. British fascination with an emergent 'Indian English' was reflected in the thousands of usages collected in *Hobson-Jobson: The Anglo-Indian Dictionary*, compiled by Yule and Burnell in 1886.

An important point to note about a multilingual country like India is that, as access to education and English varies according to economic, social and family status, the English actually used ranges from stigmatised pidgin varieties to a standard South Asian English spoken by the well educated and privileged. At the more prestigious and influential end of this continuum there is often little difference in the written form of the language between, say, an article in *The Times of India* and one in a contemporary American or British broadsheet. Occasional differences in grammar, style and idiomatic usage are certainly present, but educated South Asian English has essentially become as internationally acceptable as British or American English.

4.4 Expanding Circle: English in Japan

While the use of English in Expanding Circle territories has not yet resulted in the development of nativised varieties of English, the impact of the language can be considerable in these areas and can result in processes that give it highly distinctive forms and meanings. This is particularly true of countries like Japan, in which the native language of most of the population (Japanese) is remarkably different from English and where formal learning of English in school takes place alongside dense and creative borrowing from the language in such areas as commerce, publicity, media and sports. As in other areas of the Expanding Circle (e.g. Russia), English is not merely the main or only foreign language learnt but also plays an increasing role in social and professional life. Although most Japanese do not use English on an everyday basis, they see it all around them in the names of international companies, on office buildings, in Western-style shops and restaurants, in English-language newspapers and magazines, and can hear it in parallel with subtitles in many films and satellite TV programmes with the original soundtrack. The frequent use of words borrowed from English in Japanese reflects a widespread absorption of Western, predominantly American, cultural influences in business, advertising, pop music and fashion, etc., representing what younger Japanese may see as a more attractive image than that inscribed in their own language and culture. At the same time, however, borrowings from English are used innovatively within Japanese, and are not always transparent in sound or meaning to speakers of English from outside Japan (see examples in 4.4.1 below).

4.4.1 Borrowed words in Japanese

Japanese has traditionally been very hospitable to borrowing from other languages. This started through contact with China more than a thousand years ago, which led to Chinese characters becoming the basis for the Japanese writing system and to thousands of Chinese words entering the Japanese lexicon. Though Japan had trading contact with Western Europe as early as the 16th century, this was interrupted by a long period of no contact with European nations (except the Dutch) as a reaction against the work of missionaries, and it was not until shortly before the Meiji Restoration of 1868 that Japan reopened to the West. Modern Japanese vocabulary is made up of native words (*wago*), words from Chinese (*kango*) and words or expressions of mostly Western origin (*gairaigo*). In recent decades English has been the main source of borrowing, with an estimated 30,000 words introduced from English in the last 50 years.

Foreign words are generally written in a special script called *katakana*, which represents them in terms of Japanese syllables. Normally each consonant is followed by one vowel, with any consonant clusters broken up, and sounds not found in Japanese (such as /l/) are represented by the nearest Japanese sound, as shown in *miruku* (milk). Other examples include *kurisumasu* (Christmas), *takushi* (taxi) and *aisukurimu* (ice cream).[5] Many English borrowings are abbreviated, such as *waa puro* (word processor), *masukomi* (mass communication) and *terebi* (television). English loan words sometimes undergo semantic change, as in the case of *tarento* (talent) which has the narrower meaning of a 'TV celebrity' in Japanese, or *manshon* (mansion), which denotes a high-class block of flats rather than a large, impressive, detached house. Borrowed words from English are also often combined with Japanese words, as in *haburashi*, from Japanese *ha* (tooth) and English *brush*, or the well-known *kara oke* ('empty orchestra') which contains in *oke* an abbreviation of *orchestra*. Some English words are combined to form completely new usages known as *wasei eigo* ('made-in-Japan English'). Examples include *pureigaido* ('play guide', or ticket agency), *imejiappu* ('image up', or improving one's image) or the euphemistic *shiruba hauzingu* ('silver housing', or housing for the elderly).

4.4.2 Decorative English

Since the 1980s some borrowings from English have been used more or less simply for visual, ornamental effect, and are usually referred to as *Decorative English*. These appear on pencil cases, stationery, clothing, shopping bags and photo albums, etc., or are used as slogans for notices or advertising. As Dougill (1987) and Brock (1991) have pointed out, such English is meant, through the appearance of the *romaji* (Roman alphabet) alone, to convey an atmosphere of modern sophistication and glamour rather than to be formally accurate or to make much sense. Though the source of *Decorative English* is considered to be Japan, its use is widespread in East Asia and it has also spread through commercial activities to other countries. Examples from East Asia include the following:

Let's sport violent all day long (Japan – on a T-shirt)
My tasty time (Japan – slogan of a telephone company)
Boys Love Big Sun Shine (Hong Kong – on a blazer)

---

[5] The English origin of these words is more transparent if we note that the 'u' is pronounced very indistinctly, so that *takushi* sounds more like *tak'shi*, *kurisumasu* more like *k'ris'mas'*, and *aisukurimu* more like *ais'k'rim'*.

My boastful hot apple tea (Korea – in a notebook)
They just remember remote from place (Indonesia – on a ruler)
(The examples from Japan are taken from Dougill (1987)
and those from Hong Kong, Korea and Indonesia from Brock (1991).
They are reprinted with others in McArthur (1998:27).)

4.4.3   An Expanding Circle variety?

The interesting thing about *Decorative English* is that, although no more than a commercial fad, it illustrates sharply an important dimension of the use of English in Expanding Circle territories. It would be unwise to assume, just because most people in these areas 'officially' learn Standard American or British English in school (and in numerous private English language teaching establishments employing a large number of teachers with English as their first language), that their actual use of the language in informal contexts is more 'Inner Circle oriented' than that of speakers from Outer Circle countries using nativised varieties. And it would be equally unwise to assume that their English is necessarily accessible to speakers of English from elsewhere. *Gairaigo* and *wasei ego* (including *Decorative English*) are phenomena that have allowed the Japanese to absorb English in a way that is distinctively their own. While English is changing the Japanese language, through the absorption of a huge amount of English vocabulary, English is itself being changed in the process of diffusion and being given a strikingly new character. Arguably, in Japan, a regional variety of Expanding Circle English has got off the ground and may export its influence to other East Asian countries.

At the same time, English is under pressure from other languages in the Expanding Circle, despite its apparent dominance. Since Japan shares with China, Korea and other countries in the area a writing system of Chinese origin, Chinese could remain a rival to English as a lingua franca in this economically powerful part of the world. This could also occur in other areas, such as the Russian Federation. Here, borrowed vocabulary undergoes a process of transliteration (into Cyrillic in this case) resulting in some phonological and semantic changes not dissimilar to those happening in Japan. In addition, in this region several countries are likely, for cultural and linguistic reasons, to favour the continued use of Russian as a common language.

4.5   Summary

In this chapter we have surveyed global English from the perspectives of an Inner Circle, Outer Circle and Expanding Circle territory. In each case assumptions about the use of English, or the kind of English used, are closely connected with beliefs about power and status. Not everyone in the

Inner Circle is believed by others to speak 'good' English or to have a 'pleasant' accent, and people who speak minority languages in these territories have often been discriminated against. In the Outer Circle, English is being refashioned creatively and successfully to express postcolonial identities, yet not everyone has access to it and so it continues, in a new way, to create inequalities as well as opportunities. Finally, in the Expanding Circle, English is being absorbed into some other languages at a phenomenal rate, bringing about changes both in the languages concerned and in the sociolinguistic and cultural contexts in which they are spoken. There is also increasing evidence that special forms and uses of English, if not nativised varieties, are coming about in Expanding Circle territories. We will consider the influence of the Expanding Circle on the future of English as an international language in the final chapter of this book.

Activities

The following are suggestions for project work on some of the topics introduced in this chapter:

1. Find out as much as you can about Australian English. What social and/or regional dialects of English are spoken in Australia? What sorts of attitudes to English pronunciation and/or usage can be found among Australians? What do Australians think of other Inner Circle varieties of English?
2. Compare two texts from different postcolonial or 'new' literatures in English (e.g. a poem or short story from India and one from Africa). How are Outer Circle varieties of English represented in these texts and what language-related issues do they explore (e.g. about identities or power in bilingual or multilingual societies)? Alternatively, you might like to compare two works about the same cultural context, one written during colonial times and the other written after independence. What differences can you see between them with regard to the representation of English or other languages?
3. Investigate aspects of the role of English or the learning and teaching of English in any country of the Expanding Circle (e.g. Russia, China, Sweden).

Further Reading

A classic guide to American English is Mencken (1936). For a well-illustrated account of the origins and development of American English, including Canadian English, see Chapter 7 of McCrum, Cran and MacNeil (1986). A further overview of American English, its history and diversity, can be found in Baugh and Cable (fifth edition, 2002). Full-length studies include Wolfram and Schilling-Estes (1998), and Tottie (2002), which has detailed coverage of the formal characteristics of contemporary American English, as well as a useful chapter on features of spoken interaction. See Gupta (1999), Kachru (1983) and Kirkpatrick (2002) for more thorough accounts of, respectively, Singaporean, Indian and Asian Englishes. For more on English in Japan see Hoffer and Honna (1999), Loveday (1996) and Kubota (in Black and Cameron 2002).

Chapter 5

Ethnicity and Varieties of English

5.1 Introduction

In this chapter we turn to the relationship between ethnic affiliation and English. *Ethnicity* refers to a person's origins in terms of their race, culture and family background. The word *ethnic* is found in a very wide range of contexts today, sometimes having a blatantly racist meaning (as in the chilling *ethnic cleansing*) and sometimes being used in a general cultural sense, as when we refer to *ethnic* restaurants, jewellery, music, hairstyles and fashion. Where *ethnic* refers to people directly, the emphasis tends to be on their cultural background and the characteristics that make them distinctive. Where it refers to cuisine or fashion and so on, *ethnic* has, fundamentally, a more commercial meaning, referring to items that represent or derive from the traditions of a particular group of people and that anyone else can, if they wish, 'sample'. It is often naively assumed that *ethnic* implies *minority*, because those who belong to the *ethnic majority* or the dominant cultural group in a particular place consider their own ethnicity to be the norm and therefore it is the ethnicity of those outside the dominant group that tends to be 'marked'. The ethnicity of minority groups is marked, for example, in situations where an individual's skin colour is mentioned where this has absolutely no bearing on the context, while that of other individuals is treated as normative and not commented on.

Ethnicity can be broken down from large to smaller groups, depending on where our loyalty lies. For instance, a British person might feel a stronger allegiance to, say, Welsh ethnicity than to English, feeling that Welsh and English cultures retain a certain distinctiveness despite centuries of political union. Even Welsh people who do not speak or understand the Welsh language often identify with their cultural and geographical roots in this way, though it might be argued that those who do speak Welsh generally have a deeper sense of Welsh identity. This is because language has a central role in our sense of ethnicity and can survive beyond national borders and where the sense of national identity has been undermined or lost.

In this chapter we will look at some of the most important ways in which ethnicity has played a part in developing varieties of English, first of all considering pidgin and creole Englishes and then exploring the phenomena of African American Vernacular English and Chicano English in the light of attitudes to English in education and the impact of various powerful language lobbies.

5.2 Pidgins and creoles

One of the reasons why English has become the global language that it is today is that it has in many parts of the world been used as a *lingua franca* or common means of communication for a considerable time. In some parts of the world, especially coastal regions where contact between different groups of people began for trading purposes, English has taken on very distinctive forms, undergoing a process of simplification and hybridisation as it has been combined with features from other languages. The process whereby a dominant language (usually that of a one-time colonial power) is used alongside other local languages for practical purposes of basic trade and negotiation gives rise to a hybrid form of language called a *pidgin*. Pidgin languages are characterised by their simplification of the syntax and lexis of the contributing languages and by the fact that they are not spoken as a vernacular or native language, but used only when required for limited communicative needs between people who do not have a common language.

When a community is multilingual, however, and more and more people begin to increase their use of a pidgin as a contact language, the range of situations in which this contact language is used widens and its grammar and lexis expand and become more complex. A new generation is then likely to learn this variety as their mother tongue. When this occurs, the pidgin has become a fully functioning language and is called a *creole*. When a pidgin becomes a creole, its phonology, syntax and vocabulary all become more complex, so that it can be used effectively in all the situations in which it is the medium of communication. Examples of English-based pidgins that are now creoles include *Bislama*, used in Fiji and the Solomon Islands and an official language in Vanuatu, and *Tok Pisin* in Papua New Guinea, spoken by over two million people and widely used in commercial and administrative contexts.

5.2.1 English-based creoles

The English-based creoles of the world have many formal similarities, especially in grammatical structure. For example, the creole first used by black slaves in the Caribbean and America had a West African linguistic background, but came increasingly under the influence of English as a result of contact with a powerful, white English-speaking population. Where the pressure to move more towards a dominant parent language exists in this way, a **post-creole continuum** comes into being. At the most socially prestigious end of the continuum an **acrolect**, or variety closest to the standard dialect, is spoken by the most educated groups, while at the least prestigious end a **basilect** is used. Varieties that are placed between these two extremes are called **mesolects**. Where the acrolect develops into a powerful and institutionalised variety of English, a phase known as **decreolisation** can occur. When this happens, stigma towards the other forms of the creole will increase and they may be proscribed in official or educational contexts. This can sometimes lead to the eventual disappearance of the creole altogether, though its ultimate fate often depends on whether and in what way its speakers choose to value and defend it.

Let us look in more detail at an English-based creole, namely Jamaican Creole or Jamaican Patwa.[1] This exists as a basilect alongside the acrolectal variety of Jamaican English. Some of the most noticeable features of Jamaican Patwa are as follows:

Phonological:

- The use of the vowel /aː/ in *paw* and *card*
- The use of the vowel /a/ in *hat, hot, one*
- The use of the vowel /ɒ/ in *gun* and *but*
- The tendency not to distinguish between /t–θ/ and /d–ð/, so that *oath* is pronounced like *oat* and *though* is pronounced like *dough*.
- The use of the diphthong /ai/ for both *buy* and *boy*
- Non-rhoticity, so that the /r/ is not pronounced after a vowel, as in words like *card* and *water*. Note, however, that some Caribbean Englishes, such as those of Barbados and Guyana, are rhotic.
- The devoicing, reduction or loss of final consonant clusters: *England* becomes *Englan'*
- The rhythm of Patwa stresses every syllable more or less equally

Lexico-grammatical:

- Plurals are not generally marked with -s: *two cat, all di book*
- Possession is expressed without an apostrophe 's: *dis man coat* (this man's coat), or through the use of the particle *fi*, as in *de bok a fi me* (the book is mine).
- Subject versus object case is not necessarily distinguished in pronoun use: *She come, take she book an' read*
- Non-standard s- concord between subject and verb: *She sing every day*
- Lack of *be* as copula or auxiliary verb: *di man sad, dem coming*
- The negation of verbs through use of a *no* particle and use of multiple negation for emphasis: *he no want dat, Ain' nobody go nowhere las' week*

---

[1] Patwa, from 'patois', is a term that is sometimes used to stigmatise basilectal forms of a creole. However, in some contexts, it has been reclaimed as a badge of pride in ethnic identity, as in the case of Jamaican Patwa in Britain.

- Past tenses are expressed with the base form of the verb: *Linton go last week*. With stative verbs 'did' is often used: *She did know dem*. Completed actions in the past are expressed by 'done': *She just done tell dem*
- Continuous actions are marked with particles such as 'da', 'di' or 'a': *Linton da work now*
- Reduplication: *picky-picky* (choosy), *one one* (all alone)

Jamaican Patwa has become well known internationally through immigration of West Indians to English-speaking countries, particularly Britain, and through the significant impact of Caribbean popular culture, particularly reggae music. Many Jamaican immigrants to the UK have actively maintained the use of Patwa in informal social networks, song lyrics and poetry. Often their use of it is a badge of protest against the pressure to assimilate into the mainstream culture, or against perceived victimisation by the dominant group in areas such as education and employment.

Some of the features listed above can be seen in the following poem by Jean 'Binta' Breeze, a poet and performer who divides her time between England and Jamaica:

seasons

(for Linton)

sometime,
when im coming
is like a cole front
cross de Atlantic
or a chilling eas wind
den yuh have to meet him
ratianal,
lagical,
wid a clarity
dat is more
intellectual
but occasianally
spirit tek
an a smile
wid a twinkle
in de I
does warm de heart
like summer come in May
or tulips out in Feb
an yuh haffi sey
it did wut it
after all
fi endure im winta

(Jean 'Binta' Breeze, 2000 *The Arrival of Brighteye and Other Poems* Tarset: Bloodaxe)

This poem is a useful example of how Jamaican English creole is represented in creative writing. In it we can find much evidence of pronunciation-guided spelling, such as 'cole' for 'cold', 'de' for 'the', 'ratianal', 'lagical', 'occasianally', for 'rational', 'logical' and 'occasionally', and 'yuh' for 'you'. The use of 'I' for 'eye' in 'in de I' is less easy to explain, as 'I' and 'eye' are pronounced the same. However, the play on words here might be a means of suggesting that the 'eye' of the speaker is the centre, in some way, of her 'I-ness' or identity.[2] Creole grammar is represented in the poem by, for instance, 'wen im coming' for 'when he's coming' (or 'when he comes'), where the object pronoun 'im' ('him') performs the role of clause subject and the auxiliary verb is omitted. Immediately after this we find 'is like' for 'it's like', in which the subject is omitted. In 'spirit tek/an a smile', the definite article is dropped before 'spirit', and in 'does warm de heart' (for 'warms the heart'), we find the auxiliary 'do' being used in a declarative proposition, a non-standard feature in English in modern times. The final lines 'it did wut it/after all/fi endure im winta' might be rendered as 'it (the spirit) did what it had to do, after all, to endure his (its?) winter'. The phrase 'im winta' might at first be read as a variant of 'in winter', but this would be unlikely, as the phrases 'in May' or 'in Feb' retain the standard prepositional form 'in'. Also, case distinction between pronouns in Jamaican creole is not necessarily observed, so 'his' often occurs as 'him'. Breeze is also personifying the spirit here, so the spirit could be thought of as having endured its own metaphorical winter and come through it to a new optimism. Another grammatical feature worth noting is the use of the particle 'fi' in the last line and as part of the word 'haffi' in 'haffi sey' ('have to say'). This particle can also sometimes occur in possessive constructions, as in *De book a fi me* ('the book is mine'), but in the last line of our poem it seems to express purpose.

What will strike a careful reader of this poem is that there is some inconsistency in the extent to which creole variants are used. For example, 'have to' occurs in its standard form in 'yuh have to meet him' but in its creole form in 'yuh haffi sey'. There could be several reasons for this. It is possible that Jean 'Binta' Breeze made her choice in connection with the overall flow and rhythm of the poem, simply choosing the most appropriate variant for the line in question. It could also be the case that 'haffi' may be habitually juxtaposed (or may *collocate*) with certain verbs more frequently than with others. Or it could be argued that a writer who divides her time between England and Jamaica is inevitably going to draw on both creole and standard forms of English in her work. Breeze is also a poet who, like many other poets with Caribbean roots, often 'performs' her poetry for audiences with varying levels

[2] Crystal (1995:347) notes: 'In Rastafarian speech, *I* is considered a syllable of special, mystical significance, and often appears in unusual contexts, as in West Indian poet Dennis Scott's line 'Seals every I away from light' (*More Poem*, 1982), where there is a play on words between *I* and *eye*.'

of familiarity with Jamaican Creole English, a factor which might also indirectly influence the mix of standard and creole features in her writing.

5.2.2 Attitudes to creole

Attitudes to the use of creole can be complex within the society in which it first develops, depending on the social contexts and networks in which it is spoken, the language policies of governments and so on. DeCamp (1977) drew attention to the educational consequences of the continuum of Jamaican English (going from the basilectal creole to the Standard Jamaican English taught in schools) being linked to social class, with the Creole stigmatised as the variety used by the poor, delinquent or ignorant. More recently, a study by Wassink (1999) of speakers from a semi-rural community outside Kingston, Jamaica, showed that such negative feelings towards the Creole may be losing some of their force and that younger speakers have more positive attitudes towards it and to its function in the community. However, Wassink's respondents in general retained ambivalent attitudes towards the creole variety or, to use the term adopted for it locally, the 'patois'.

A further level of complexity is added, with regard to attitudes, when a creole is 'exported' from its place of origin to another area of the world through emigration. When this takes place, the Creole speakers have to take new linguistic bearings and decide how they wish to relate to a new standard variety (e.g. the attitude to British English of Jamaican Creole speakers who have emigrated to London) and the other regional and social varieties they encounter in their adopted country. As Sebba (1993) has shown, some young British African Caribbeans have 're-creolised' their English as 'London Jamaican' with forms that differ from those of Jamaican English in Jamaica (e.g. with a Cockney pronunciation of 'through' as /fru/ rather than the Jamaican pronunciation /tru/).[3] Their aim in doing so is to assert their ethnic identity within the British context – the use of London Jamaican or British Black English thus has covert prestige as, despite its divergence from Standard British English, it represents the distinctiveness of its speakers as an ethnic group and reinforces their solidarity.

As Kramsch (1998:70) has noted, 'One way of surviving culturally in immigration settings is to exploit, rather than stifle, the endless variety of meanings afforded by participation in several discourse communities at once.' This means code-switching as an act of identification, through which speakers can reinforce cultural group membership or distance in subtle and creative ways. In fact it can involve not just code-switching, but also the stylisation of a single variety or creation of a hybrid variety of the same code. It can also reveal multiple cultural memberships by speakers who

---

[3] This process of re-creolisation by youths of West Indian origin was also noticed in earlier studies by Edwards (1986) and Hewitt (1986).

parody or stereotype different codes or styles depending on the communicative context and their interlocutors. The following shows a stylisation of both Asian and Creole English by Pakistani school pupils as an act of resistance to their teacher (BR below) in a British school:

BR: attention gents
Asif: yeh alright
Alan: alright
Asif: yeh
Kazim: (in Stylized Asian English) I AM VERY SORRY BEN JAAD
/aɪ æm veri sɒri ben dʒaːd/
Asif: (in Stylized Asian English) ATTENTION BENJAMIN
/əthenʃaːn bendʒəmɪn/
. . .
BR: concentrate a little bit
. . .
Kazim: (in Creole English) stop moving **dat ting aroun**
/dæt tɪŋ əɹɑʊn/
(from Rampton 1995:115–6)

There is evidence that Patwa is being strategically borrowed by some young white and Asian people in Britain, a claim first made by Hewitt (1986) with reference to east London youth clubs.[4] Rampton (1995) found that the occasional use of creole in a multi-ethnic context by an 'outgroup' of white and Asian adolescents was associated with their positive perception of creole in terms of youth and class identity. It was the creole-speaking group who were considered by Rampton's informants to have the greatest influence on the vernacular used in this multi-racial setting, introducing new words, for instance, that the other groups would adopt in order to move towards this leading group.

5.3 African American Vernacular English (AAVE)

Spoken by many people of African ancestry in the United States, African American Vernacular English, or AAVE (pronounced /ɑːveɪ/ or /ɑːvi/), has many characteristics that can be found across different regions, so that most linguists agree that this is a distinct ethnic variety, even though it is not spoken by *all* black people in the United States.[5] Well-educated black speakers from more privileged socio-economic classes do not necessarily use AAVE features in their own speech and may also have more ambivalent

---

[4] In particular, this phenomenon may be noticeable among some young Asian and white people in multi-ethnic areas of Britain, such as the Midlands (see Stockwell, 2002:45–46).
[5] About 80–90 per cent of the black population of the US are thought to use AAVE, the majority coming from inner-city and working-class backgrounds. However, those black speakers who do not generally use the variety are still familiar with it and capable of using it if they wish to.

attitudes towards this variety. Younger speakers, however, are more likely than older speakers to use AAVE as a badge of peer-group solidarity.

Tottie (2002:227) outlines as follows the current theories about the origins of AAVE and why it differs from Standard and other varieties of English:

1 AAVE is descended from a *creole*, itself derived from an English-based *pidgin*, i.e. a contact language.
2 AAVE is a dialect of English based on the varieties that the slaves picked up from white speakers.
3 AAVE is derived from West African languages. Those who advocate this theory are often the same people who use the term *Ebonics*.

Tottie notes that the third theory is not 'accepted by professional linguists but it has had some important political consequences', as we shall see below when we discuss AAVE in the context of educational policy. As for the first and second theories, Tottie explains that there is evidence in favour of both positions. For example, the aspect system of AAVE and its African loanwords tend to support the 'creolist' theory, while evidence that black slaves might have picked up the dialects of Southern white farm employees tends to favour the position of the 'dialectologists'. The fact that AAVE is treated as a variety in its own right, whether dialectal in origin or creole-based, could be said to show that it has followed its own course, at least, and that more research will be needed to establish exactly how it has developed.

5.3.1 Linguistic features of AAVE

In its phonology AAVE shares some features with Southern US English, such as the use of the monophthong /a/ rather than the diphthong /aɪ/ in words like *hide*, *I* and *time*, especially before voiced consonants. Like Southern White English, AAVE also often merges the short vowels /e/ and /ɪ/ before nasals, losing the phonemic distinction between words like *ten* and *tin*. AAVE differs from Standard English more noticeably in its consonant system, however. It is *r*-less or non-rhotic, losing post-vocalic *r* both word-finally and before a consonant, as in *door* and *short*. Tottie (2002) also notes that intervocalic *r* can be absent, so that *Carol* sounds like *Cal*. Another distinctive feature is the reduction of word-final clusters (through the loss of the final consonant) in words like *rest*, *child*, *cold* (pronounced as if spelled *res'*, *chil'* and *col'*), although this does not apply where there is a cluster of voiced followed by voiceless consonants, as in *felt* or *pump*. Where cluster reductions occur, they can also influence morphology, as when the plural of *test* (pronounced in AAVE as /tes/) follows the rule for nouns like *kiss* and is pronounced /tesɪz/.

The pronunciation of dental fricatives depends on whether they occur initially, medially or finally in a word. The initial /ð/ in words like *the*, *this* and *them* becomes /d/, so that these words sound like *de*, *dis* and *dem*. In medial position, however, the voiced fricative is often replaced by /v/, so that *brother* may be pronounced as if written *bruvver*. The voiceless fricative may be pronounced as a /t/ initially, but sometimes occurs as /f/ in medial position, so that *thing* is pronounced like *ting*, while *nothing* often occurs as *nuf'n* (though *nut'n* is also possible).

Other phonological features include some vocalisation of /l/, so that *I'll go* and *I go* are likely to sound the same, the pronunciation of final *-ing* in words like *dancing* as /n/ rather than /ŋ/, usually shown in spelling as *dancin'*, and the reversal of some consonant sequences (metathesis), so that, for example, *ask* is pronounced like the word *axe*.

Aspects of the rhythm and intonation of AAVE are also distinctive. One rhythmical feature that is often reflected in written representations of the variety is the deletion of the first syllable in words like *about* or *remember*, shown as *'bout* and *'member*.

Among the grammatical characteristics of AAVE the aspect system of the verb phrase is the most interesting area of difference from Standard English or other vernacular US dialects. The verb *be* is frequently deleted both as a copula (except in the first person) and auxiliary form, so *she's a teacher* is expressed in the form *she a teacher* and *she's going to stay* as *she gonna stay*. When indicating that something is a habit or happens frequently, AAVE makes use of an invariant form of *be*, so that *the place is often cold* is expressed in the form *the place be cold*. In AAVE there is a contrast in aspect between the forms *subject + be + verb-ing* and *subject + verb-ing* without *be*: for example, *she be singin'* means 'she often sings', whereas *she singin'* means 'she's singing now'. Aspectual meanings of the past tense forms are also distinctive in AAVE. Some examples, with Standard English versions in brackets, include the following:

> *He done gone* ('He went recently')
> *He been gone* ('He went a long time ago')

The future is expressed by *will* but this is usually absent in contracted forms because of the common vocalisation of *l* mentioned above. The future perfect tense formed in Standard English by *will have + past participle* (e.g. 'he will have finished his work') is rendered in AAVE as *he be done finished his work*. Finally, other common features include the following:

- Non-standard subject–verb agreement (e.g. *they is here*; *he don't sing*).
- Frequent use of *ain't* in forming negative clauses, along with the use of two or more negatives in the same clause (*you ain't got time*; *ain't got no money*). Sometimes the subject pronoun is omitted in negative clauses, as in *ain't got no money*.
- Inversion of subject and auxiliary in a declarative clause when the subject is a negative word like 'nothing' or 'nobody' (*Didn't nobody see him*: 'Nobody saw him'; *Wasn't nobody there*: 'Nobody was there').

- In existential sentences, *there* is often missing and replaced by *it* (*it's a car outside*: 'There's a car outside').

The vocabulary of AAVE is characterised by a number of words of African origin (e.g. *juke, okra, tote, banjo*) and by words from English used with new meanings by black speakers (e.g. *bad* for 'good', *uptight* for 'anxious', *jive* for 'insincere talk'). Such terms are also widely adopted by white speakers, especially younger people, as they have become widely known through rap music and international popular culture.

It is important to remember that AAVE is recognised not simply by the kinds of linguistic features noted above, but also by certain identifiable discourse strategies and speaking styles. Called in Smitherman (1995) the African American Verbal Tradition (AVT), these strategies can be found, for instance, in the speech of influential political and social figures who are bidialectal as a result of their upbringing in AAVE-speaking communities (e.g. Reverend Jesse Jackson). AAVE discourse style is marked by intonation, address systems, the use of tag questions and so on, and is closely associated with the signalling of solidarity within the African American community. As Lippi-Green (1997:177–178) has pointed out:

> . . . even when no grammatical, phonological, or lexical features of AAVE are used, a person can, *in effect*, still be speaking AAVE by means of AVT rhetorical devices. Thus, while the core grammatical features of AAVE may be heard most consistently in poorer black communities where there are strong social and communication networks, AAVE phonology (particularly intonation) and black rhetorical style are heard, on occasion, from prominent and successful African Americans in public forums.

Before we consider attitudes to AAVE within education, where it has been a source of considerable controversy, I think it is worth discussing for a moment the representation of this variety in written form. As in the case of all non-standard dialects of English, when AAVE is represented in literary writing, authors try to echo its formal and rhetorical features by exploiting the resources of spelling and punctuation in unconventional ways. In the 19th and early 20th centuries, many African Americans wrote nostalgic dialect verses that mythologised the Southern past. While the following example, an extract from a poem by Paul Laurence Dunbar (1872–1906), avoids an overtly racial theme, its use of an AAVE-speaking persona has the immediate effect of appealing to African American solidarity. The servant speaker's nostalgia for the 'gospel' singing of 'Malindy' is not a direct comment on AAVE itself, but since African American singing and speech, especially in church communities, are closely interrelated (AAVE speech is highly 'musical' in its intonation patterns), so the singing referred to in the poem seems to acquire a symbolic dimension. To the narrator, its quality can never be replicated by the singing of a white singer, in this case her young Southern charge, Miss Lucy:

G'way an' quit dat noise, Miss Lucy –
   Put dat music book away;
What's de use to keep on tryin'?
   Ef you practice twell you're gray,
You cain't sta't no notes a-flyin'
   Like de ones dat rants and rings
F'om de kitchen to de big woods
   When Malindy sings.

You ain't got de nachel o'gans
   Fu' to make de soun' come right,
You ain't got de tu'ns an' twistin's
   Fu' to make it sweet an' light.
Tell you one thing now, Miss Lucy,
   An' I'm tellin' you fu' true,
When hit comes to raal right singin',
   'Tain't no easy thing to do.

Easy 'nough fu' folks to hollah,
   Lookin' at de lines an' dots,
When dey ain't no one kin sence it,
   An' de chune comes in in spots;
But fu' real melojous music,
   Dat jes' strikes yo' hawt and clings,
Jes' you stan' an' listen wif me,
   When Malindy sings.

Ain't you nevah heerd Malindy?
   Blessed soul, take up de cross!
Look heah, ain't you jokin', honey?
   Well, you don't know what you los'.
Y'ought to heah dat gal a-wa'blin',
   Robins, la'ks an' all dem things,
Heish dey moufs an' hides dey faces
   When Malindy sings.[6]

(From 'When Malindy Sings', by Paul Laurence Dunbar,
in Joan R. Sherman, ed. 1997 *African-American Poetry: An Anthology,
1773–1927* New York: Dover Publications)

[6] 'Go away and quit that noise, Miss Lucy –/Put that music book away;/What's the use of keeping on trying?/ If you practise till you're grey, /You can't [won't] start any notes flying/ Like the ones that rant and ring/ From the kitchen to the big woods/When Malindy sings. You haven't got the natural organs/To make the sound come [out] right,/You haven't got the tunes and twistings/To make it sweet and light./ [I'll] tell you one thing now, Miss Lucy,/ And I'm telling you for true,/When it comes to real, right singing,/ it isn't an easy thing to do. [It's] easy enough for folks to hollah [shout],/Looking at the lines and dots,/When there isn't anyone who can make sense of it,/ And the tune [only] comes in in spots;/But for real melodious music,/That just strikes your heart and clings,/Just you stand and listen with me,/ When Malindy sings. Haven't you ever heard Malindy?/ Blessed soul, take up the cross!/ Look hear, aren't you joking, honey?/Well, you don't know what you've lost./ You ought to hear that girl warbling,/Robins, larks and all those things,/Hush their mouths and hide their faces/When Malindy sings.'

In this poem we can find a number of the features of AAVE already mentioned. In the first two verses, for example, we find the spelling 'dat' for 'that' and 'de' for 'the', reflecting the pronunciation of the voiced dental fricative. The spelling of 'sta't' (for 'start') represents a non-rhotic pronunciation of the word. Another feature is the loss of 'g' in, for example, 'tryin'', where the second syllable would be pronounced /ɪn/ rather than /ɪŋ/. Syllables are deleted in 'twell' for 'until' and 'nachel' for 'natural', and there is consonant cluster reduction in 'F'om' ('From') and 'soun''. Typical AAVE negative constructions are seen in 'You cain't sta't no notes a-flyin'' and "Tain't no easy thing to do'. (The last two verses of this poem will not be commented on here, as they are the focus of one of the Activities at the end of the chapter.)

5.3.2 Attitudes to AAVE

Before looking at attitudes to AAVE specifically, we need to consider the broader picture of language attitudes in the United States, particularly with regard to education and notions of American citizenship. The latter half of the 20th century saw considerable debate among educators, linguists and the public on the relationship between English and other languages spoken in the US, as well as between Standard English and non-standard varieties of the language. In 1981 Senator Hayakawa of California proposed an *English Language Amendment* to the Constitution to make it the official language of the United States. Though the proposal was not approved by the Senate, Hayakawa co-founded an organisation called *US English* in 1983 which still lobbies for the Amendment and for 'Official English' at state level in almost all government and public meetings, documents and legislation. Another organisation, *English First*, which was established in 1986, shares the same aims, but in addition campaigns against bilingual schooling and voting. These organisations justify their conservative stance with the argument that US citizens of all backgrounds should be assimilated into one shared sense of national identity, and that speaking English is essential if this is to happen.

Not surprisingly, several other organisations have been set up to counter the influence of these groups. The most well known is *English Plus*, founded in 1987, which opposes the English Language Amendment and supports the development of bilingual education in schools, as well as wider provision of social services in languages other than English. *English Plus* and other groups that oppose 'Official English' policies believe that, far from ensuring national cohesion, they would fuel intolerance towards ethnic and linguistic minority groups.

AAVE has been caught up in this debate because in December 1996 the Oakland school board in California issued a resolution which was understood to imply that African Americans spoke a separate language, not a dialect of English, and could therefore qualify for bilingual education grants. This was the position supported by campaigners for *Ebonics* (a term for AAVE blending 'ebony' and 'phonics' favoured by those who link it with African languages), so it became known as the 'Ebonics controversy'. However, during much heated public debate, linguists clarified that AAVE is not a language in its own right, but a variety of English, and so could not be treated in the same way as other minority languages in the US, such as Chinese and Russian. The Oakland board decided to omit the word *Ebonics* from a revised proposal in April 1997.

Attitudes to AAVE among African Americans are often ambivalent. Lippi-Green (1997:185) writes that 'it is hard to find any African American, regardless of profession, politics, or personal belief, who would deny the practical necessity of bidialectalism and selective assimilation to MUSE [Mainstream US English] norms'. However, while the majority of African Americans seem to accept that assimilation to MUSE norms is hard to resist in some contexts, they can also be suspicious of those who adopt Standard English too readily. As Lippi-Green points out, the debate often centres itself too narrowly on attitudes towards discrete formal issues of Standard English proficiency (especially subject-verb agreement), whereas AAVE discourse strategies and intonation (often detectable in the speech of successful African Americans who have assimilated to MUSE norms) receive insufficient attention. Lippi-Green highlights this, because there is evidence that these too are sometimes stigmatised, especially by non-black MUSE speakers, who 'have a much lower tolerance for non-grammatical features of AAVE than some seem to realize' (Lippi-Green 1997:200).

5.4 Chicano English

People of Mexican, Puerto Rican, Cuban and other Spanish-speaking backgrounds in the US are ethnically grouped together as 'Hispanics'.[7] In the 1990 US Census 60 per cent of Hispanics reported their national origin as Mexican, and it has been estimated that Mexican-American English, or Chicano English, is now spoken by around 25 to 30 million people in the US (Baugh and Cable, 2002:385).

5.4.1 Linguistic features of Chicano English

Chicano English differs from Standard American English mainly in pronunciation. Here is a selection (adapted from Tottie 2002:228–229) of some of the main segmental differences:

---

[7] Note that this term has been criticised for its lack of applicability to a large proportion of the population of Mexico and Central America who have other ethnic backgrounds, such as *mestizo* (mixed European and Native American ancestry) and groups who speak no Spanish at all. See Lippi-Green (1997:229–230).

- Loss of distinction between /tʃ/ and /ʃ/, so *choose* and *shoes* may sound the same.
- Devoicing of /z/ to /s/, so *spies* sounds like *spice*.
- In word-final position /v/ is pronounced like /f/, e.g. *live* (adjective) is pronounced like *life*.
- In other positions /v/ is pronounced like /b/ in words like *never* and *fever*.
- Initial /dʒ/ becomes /j/, so *just* is pronounced /jas/.
- /h/ becomes /χ/ in *hit, whole*.
- consonant clusters are reduced, so *it's* is pronounced /ɪs/.
- /e/ is lengthened in words like *intention, send*.
- /i/ is shortened to /ɪ/ in words like *feel* and *weak*.

Other characteristics include the tendency to stress the final element in compounds (e.g. *police de'partment* rather than *po'lice department*) and to use a rising, rather than falling, intonation for statements.

Although these features are typical, they are not necessarily used to the same degree by every speaker of Chicano English. Baugh and Cable point out that '[w]hile features of pronunciation and intonation may remain stable, the selection of those features depends on numerous variables, including the context of speech and the attitude of the speaker' (2002:385). This is because the community of speakers of this variety is a rather complex one, spanning those who are bilingual in Spanish and English, those who are more proficient in one language than the other and those who may simply have acquired Chicano English as their first language. Bilingual speakers frequently code-switch between English and Spanish, a characteristic extensively illustrated in the work of writers such as Rolando Hinojosa.

5.4.2 Attitudes to Chicano English

While Chicano American and Latino American English have established their own literatures, attitudes to Hispanic speakers of English in the US have often been discriminatory. Despite its diversity, the Latino population has tended to be constructed in popular culture as a homogenous community that refuses to learn English or speaks inferior or inadequate English. The label *Spanglish* (for code-switching between Spanish and English) has often been used to undermine the linguistic identities of Hispanics by not taking the natural linguistic behaviour of bilinguals seriously. As Lippi-Green writes (1997:234):

> There is a shorthand at work here, and that is, there is only one acceptable choice: it is not enough for Spanish speakers to become bilingual; they must learn the *right* English – and following from that, the right US culture, into which they must assimilate completely.

This kind of discrimination has also been reinforced by negative stereotyping of Mexican Americans in popular culture: they have all too frequently been portrayed as dealers in violence, drugs and corruption. Though in more recent years Spanish-speaking Americans have had increasing influence on US society and politics, this does not mean that negative attitudes towards Latino use of English, particularly in terms of accent, have been overcome.

Nonetheless, Hispanic English is having an increasingly noticeable influence on mainstream US English and other Inner Circle Englishes in terms of the lexicon. Borrowed words noted in Baugh and Cable (2002:386) include *nachos*, *sangria*, *margarita* in the food and drink category, and *Sandinista*, *Contra* and *Fidelist* from politics. We can expect the growing contact between Spanish and English in the US to be a source of many more such borrowings in the future, some of which are likely to become known and used across the English-speaking world.

5.4 Summary

In this chapter we have seen that the relationship between ethnicity and variation in English is a highly sensitive one. While English pidgin languages may evolve into rich and highly effective creoles, not all creole languages based on English have survived the pressure to standardise towards international norms. The attitudes, not only of educationalists and policy-makers, but of ordinary speakers, determine how far a variety of English associated with a minority or generally less powerful ethnic group will be supported in schools, workplaces and communities. In multi-ethnic contexts, more tolerant attitudes can often be found. Evidence of strategic code switching by school pupils in multi-cultural educational settings shows that Standard English norms are not necessarily preferred or advantageous, especially within youth culture, though not all teachers are prepared or sufficiently trained to deal with code-switching in the classroom. Finally, the way a variety of English such as AAVE or Chicano English is represented in literature and popular culture is an indication of prevailing attitudes towards it, attitudes both of those who represent it and of their intended and implied audiences.

Activities

1. Look again at the last two verses of 'When Malindy Sings' by Paul Laurence Dunbar. With the help of the list of selected features of AAVE provided in this chapter and also the 'translation' in footnote 6, see how many different characteristics of AAVE you can identify.
2. Find a short poem written in Creole English (e.g. a poem by Linton Kwesi Johnson or Benjamin Zephaniah) and write a 'translation' of it in

Standard English. Read the two versions through, one after the other. What effect do you think this 're-coding' has on the impact and effectiveness of the poem?

3. If you have access to people who use AAVE or Chicano English, or any other variety of English associated with a particular ethnic group, devise a questionnaire to ask them about their attitudes towards their own language use and towards Standard English.

Further Reading

Lippi-Green (1997) includes an excellent chapter on 'Black English', as well as a very helpful section on attitudes towards Hispanic cultures and language use. See also Smitherman (1999) on African American language and culture. Tottie (2002) contains accessible and well-illustrated chapters on varieties of American English and on US language politics. Sebba (1993) is a detailed study of 'London Jamaican'. There are many book-length studies of pidgins and creoles available, but for informative shorter introductions see Holmes (2001) or Wardhaugh (2002).

Chapter 6

Gender, Sexuality and English

6.1   Introduction

In this chapter we will turn to what is a rather complex area of variation in English. Gender and sexuality are, first of all, difficult to relate in simple terms to language use. Whereas we can say that someone born and brought up in a particular area of the country is likely to speak with a particular accent or dialect, it is not possible to say that someone who is female is likely to speak 'female' English, as if this were a clearly definable and describable 'variety' of the language. Of course, certain physiological differences between female and male speech organs do result in a different natural pitch range for the voice, a phenomenon often exploited by comedians when they exaggeratedly mimic the voice qualities of the opposite sex. However, these physiological differences affect merely the 'sound' of women's and men's voices, not the linguistic choices they make, for example, with regard to words and grammatical structure. And although, as we shall see below, research has isolated some typically female and male speech habits in English, these are not inevitable occurrences in the speech of any particular woman or man in a given communicative context. Indeed, linguistic features thought typical of male speech in English can sometimes be found in female speech, and vice versa, so it is dangerous to oversimplify the relationship between gender and the language.

As children we learn the social and cultural norms for our biological sex in terms of codes of dress and general behaviour, and also begin to learn how language plays a part in constructing, representing, reinforcing and sometimes contesting those norms. As we develop an awareness of our gender and sexuality, we are likely to become more conscious of the gender-related aspects of our use of English. The language then becomes an arena in which gender and sexuality are, alongside the arenas of dress and social behaviour, more consciously enacted or 'performed'.

This chapter will look quite closely at the notion of gender *performativity* through English. However, first we need to consider to what extent formal aspects of English today can be considered imbalanced with regard to gender and to look at some of the ways in which perceived imbalances have been challenged.

6.2 Word forms and meanings

Old English was an inflected language, as German or French, for instance, continue to be today. This meant that many of its words had inflections or endings added to them to signal their grammatical class or function. Nouns, as well as articles and adjectives, took forms that indicated whether they were masculine, feminine or neuter, as well as what their function in the clause was (nominative, accusative, genitive or dative). Modern English has lost most of these inflected forms. Adjectives no longer have different forms for agreeing with the nouns to which they refer. Nearly all nouns are now uninflected for gender, though gender is still revealed in some nouns retaining gendered suffixes like *actor*, *fireman* and *headmaster*. Nowadays *actor* is often the preferred choice to refer to females as well as males who act, but *actress* continues to be used. The gender-neutral alternatives *firefighter* and *headteacher* have in many English-speaking contexts replaced *fireman* and *headmaster*. With many pairs of nouns, such as *manager* and *manageress*, the male form is the unmarked or 'original' form and the female marked, that is, the form that is appended to the male. It is clear that the female form is the appended form here, as it cannot exist without the preceding male suffix. In other words, we can go from *manage* to *manager* but not from *manage* to **managess*; we have to create the male form first and then add the female suffix. Another problem with paired nouns has to do with an imbalance in their connotations. For example, in *host* and *hostess* we find quite a different range of meanings for each form. Although both can mean someone who entertains invited guests, *hostess* can also mean a woman who welcomes and entertains customers at a nightclub (a semantic derogation or disparagement even more striking in the pair *master* and *mistress*) and is the only form that occurs before a well-known *trolley* that keeps cooked food warm. No city has ever been *hostess* to the Olympic Games nor any region *hostess* to some of the world's rarest flora and fauna. Continuing the trend to reserve *host* for what we might loosely call more 'important' or 'powerful' meanings, it is only *host* that can occur before *computer*. Sometimes the degree of semantic derogation within the female counterpart of some pairs of nouns, such as *bachelor* and *spinster*, is such that the female form has gone out of general use. *Spinster* goes back to the 14th century and used to mean a woman who made her living from spinning yarn. In Early Modern English it was used to designate the formal status of a woman who was unmarried, a usage which survives in some legal and religious contexts (as in the phrase *spinster of this parish*). However, during the 20th century the term began to be used to allude to a stereotype of an older unmarried woman assumed to be childless, prissy and repressed, which has now resulted in its being labelled in dictionaries as an offensive term. Interestingly, the more positive connotations of the word *bachelor* (e.g. in the term *eligible bachelor*) have been used by young, single, North American women in the terms *bachelor girl* and *bachelorette*. These terms, despite the gender-marking implied in adding 'girl' or the suffix '-ette', are intended to describe confident single women who feel they are in no way less independent than their male counterparts. They represent a conscious rather than automatic use of gender-marking in a spirit, not of compliance and subordination, but of feminist assertiveness. However, *bachelor girl* fails to rectify the imbalance of the pair *bachelor* and *spinster*, as it connects female singlehood with carefree youth rather than with female choice regardless of age. An older unmarried woman is not likely to be referred to as a *bachelor girl*, whereas an older unmarried man can still be a *bachelor*.

There are a few cases where it is the male and not the female counterpart that is marked. *Male prostitute* exists because the unmarked term *prostitute* is automatically taken to refer to a woman. Whether or not being the unmarked term in this case confers any power or superiority on the female is debatable and perhaps irrelevant, given the fact that prostitution is, in most societies, a socially stigmatised way of earning a living. Another example of a marked form to denote the male is *male nurse*, a result of the fact that nurses have traditionally been female. Recently there was some discussion in Britain about what male nurses would be called if, as was planned, the role of *matron* were reintroduced as the senior nursing position in a ward.

6.3 Generic meaning

Another kind of imbalance occurs in words intended or assumed to have a generic meaning, referring to both females and males, but which in fact often fail to do so. The use of *man* in a generic sense is a case in point. In *Man cannot live by bread alone* it does mean *human beings*, but the fact that *man* is also the word used for a person of the male sex can prove problematical in other apparently generic uses of the word. In many common expressions and idioms containing the word *man* the gender-specific meaning undermines the generic meaning, because only male persons are really implied. This can be shown by trying to use these expressions to refer to females. For instance, could we say without a sense of awkwardness *She's as ambitious as the next man*? While *men in grey suits* might be an apt description of many powerful figures at the top of large organisations, it makes us think of male figures and not female, despite the fact that nowadays an increasing number of board members are female. Similarly, when scientists or psychiatrists are described as *men in white coats*, we imagine males and are encouraged to think of science as a male preserve. When researchers interview *the man in the street*, again it is a male and not a female respondent that the idiom invites us to picture. Such expressions are, of course, a sign that knowledge, power and activity outside the home have traditionally been associated with men and not women. When first used, their privileging of male persons would have been seen as nothing more than a straightforward reflection of the natural order.

The generic use of *man* has also meant that the corresponding pronoun *he* has also traditionally had a dual function of both referring to a specific male person and, ostensibly, to persons of both sexes. In *Ask the buyer for his signature* it might be intended that the buyer could be male or female, but the male is privileged. The alternative of *Ask the buyer for his or her signature* makes allowance for female customers, but the sequence *his or her* implicitly makes the female secondary. It is also awkward when repeated several times within the same sentence, as in this example from a 'Terms and Conditions of Employment' booklet for academic staff:

> The Head of the Department will be asked to state in his/her reports if he/she has any grounds for thinking he/she may not be able to recommend eventual confirmation of the appointment.

Despite the apparent effort to allow for the possibility that the Head of Department could be female, the sequencing of the pronouns automatically associates the 'he', and not the 'she', more closely with the subject of each clause and therefore, for all the good intentions, reinforces the notion of a male-dominated workplace. Admittedly, this use of *he or she* is sometimes challenged through reversing the pronouns (note my own use of 'women and men' and 'female and male' in this chapter), but this usage is still found more in writing than in speech. The replacement of generic *he* with *s/he* is another alternative that can apply only to written English. The usage that solves these problems most equitably is the adoption of the plural pronoun or, where possible, the use of a plural noun as subject of the clause:

> *Every student is expected to see their tutor by the second week of term.*
> Or
> *Students are expected to see their tutor by the second week of term.*

Although some commentators might object to the lack of grammatical concord between the singular subject and the plural possessive pronoun in the first example, this usage is justifiable on grounds of fairness and is not the only instance of usage where concord is ignored (and in everyday conversation native speakers of English often make mistakes with grammatical concord which they are unaware of or do not usually bother to correct). A well-known point of comparison is the common use, at least in British English, of a plural verb with a singular subject denoting a collective of people, such as *the government* or *the committee*. In *The committee are in some disagreement on whether to admit more members*, the lack of agreement between subject and verb enables us to view *the committee* as a group of separate individuals with opinions of their own. We might like to contrast this with *The committee is supporting the introduction of a website*, where the joint stance of the committee members is what matters. The distinction, however, is by no means a rule, and usage in this area tends to be dictated more by personal preference or habit than anything else. In the case of *Every student is expected to see their tutor by the second week of term*, however, the use of *their* draws considerably less attention to gender than *his or her*, or *her or his*, taking it more for granted, perhaps, that both sexes are well represented within the student populations of the Western world (if not equally well within all academic disciplines). Whether we choose to say *their* in this context or not will therefore convey a subtly different signal about our attitudes and the degree to which we want to influence others' use of English with regard to gender-neutrality.

There is one further aspect of words and gender that we should consider before moving on to the characteristics of female and male talk: the question of whether female English speakers use particular words more frequently than male speakers. In an influential study Robin Lakoff (1975) suggested that women's speech was characterised by, among other features, the use of more precise colour terms, like *magenta* or *aquamarine*. Women have not been shown actually to perceive colours more acutely than men, so the fact that they tend to use more specific colour terms is likely to be due to the influence of traditional female jobs and activities. This is comparable to the general assumption that most men have wider 'technical' vocabularies than most women and also larger lexicons in relation to certain sports, like boxing and football. Differences in these areas, however, depend on the extent to which the association of the one or other gender with specific areas of activity remains stable. In Britain and America women's football appears to be gaining popularity, so it is likely that some younger females are acquiring greater familiarity with the sport and its lexicon. Lakoff also suggested that women used intensifiers like *just* and *so* more frequently than men, arguing that these were 'boosting devices' that indirectly signalled a lack of confidence on the part of the speaker. The question of speaker confidence, however, takes us beyond words and is central to the next section, where we will look more closely at the way gender is constructed in talk and social discourse.

6.4 Gender, talk and discourse

When we turn from words to conversational interaction, the issues we need to consider are whether women and men talk in different ways and, if so, what might bring the differences about. We need to investigate the role of power and solidarity in relation to female and male speech, and to broaden our perspective to take account of gender performance through language, where speech stereotypes may be deliberately exploited to blur gender boundaries. Moving from talk to social discourse, we also need to give some consideration to the ways in which gender is constructed in domains such as the fashion industry, which have an important impact on how individuals understand the nature of their identities as gendered beings.

6.4.1 Dominance

There is a great deal of 'folklore' about the ways in which women and men typically talk and this has, to a certain extent, affected even formal research into aspects of gender and conversation. For instance, in the 1960s and 1970s sociolinguists like Labov in the US and Trudgill in Britain tended to interpret women's linguistic behaviour as evidence of their assumed subordinate social roles, taking the traditional family as the main unit of social stratification. This 'dominance' view resulted in suggestions that women were more status-conscious than men (because they in fact had lower status themselves) and that they used more careful pronunciation and fewer non-standard or socially disfavoured forms. Trudgill (1972) argued that men's greater use of non-standard speech could be seen in terms of masculine solidarity, especially as constructed within the traditional working class. Thus, for men of this socio-economic group, such speech had covert prestige. Subsequent research by Milroy (1980) looked more closely at the influence of social networks on this variable in a study of three neighbourhoods in Belfast. One of these, Ballymacarrett, showed a sharp division between the social network patterns of males and females, the females having low network strength by comparison with the males, who were employed in the local shipyard and spent their free time together in local pubs and clubs. By contrast, the women were mostly employed outside the local area and did not form such a close-knit group. The strength of the male networks resulted in the men's far greater use of local and non-standard speech, while the much looser networks of the women made them model their language more on general, higher status norms. Such research reinforced the need to consider contexts of language use more closely when investigating the phenomenon of female speech and 'correctness'. From a feminist linguistic point of view, women's preference for standard forms could be seen as an indication of rebellion against the 'vernacular' forms associated with a more traditional patriarchal order, rather than an indirect sign of women's lower status or their respect for standard language in the context of child-rearing. It is interesting that writers of fiction in English have often given their male characters stronger regional accents than the female characters, which suggests not only that the woman has traditionally been seen as a custodian of 'good' language in the home, especially the working-class home, but that she was capable of using her 'better' language to her own advantage at times, for example, in expressing her own views more effectively. Consider, for example, the following fictional dialogue between an East Midlands coalminer and his wife (about their son's decision to enlist in the army):

She got ready and went by the first train to Derby, where she saw her son and the sergeant. It was, however, no good.

When Morel was having his dinner in the evening, she said suddenly: 'I've had to go to Derby today.'

The miner turned up his eyes, showing the whites in his black face.

'Has ter, lass. What took thee there?'

'That Arthur!'

'Oh – an' what's agate now?'

'He's only enlisted.'

Morel put down his knife and leaned back in his chair.

'Nay,' he said, 'that he niver 'as!'

'And is going down to Aldershot tomorrow.'

'Well!' exclaimed the miner. 'That's a winder.' He considered it a moment, said 'H'm!' and proceeded with his dinner. Suddenly his face contracted with wrath. 'I hope he may never set foot i' my house again,' he said.

'The idea!' cried Mrs Morel. 'Saying such a thing!'

'I do,' repeated Morel. 'A fool as runs away for a soldier, let 'im look after 'issen; I s'll do no more for 'im.'

'A fat sight you have done as it is,' she said.

And Morel was almost ashamed to go to his public-house that evening.

(D.H. Lawrence, 2003 *Sons and Lovers* London: Penguin)

In this short extract we can see that Mrs Morel does not accommodate to her husband's regional dialect speech at all. Indeed, she openly criticises what he says ('Saying such a thing!') and, even when angered, continues to use a fairly standard English idiom in telling her husband sarcastically he has done a 'fat sight' (i.e. a 'fat lot' or minimal amount) for his son anyway. Mrs Morel is indeed more aware of language and social status than her husband, but she also maintains standard forms as a means of linguistic resistance to what she clearly regards as his unfeeling and uncouth world, rather than simply for decorum's sake.

6.4.2 Difference

The 'dominance' view of gender and speech styles presented a problem in that it tended to generalise male speakers as inevitably and deliberately dominant and female speakers as inevitably weaker and more subordinate. Its observations were hardly neutral and objective, since it took male speech as the norm against which to judge female speech. Deborah Tannen (1990) challenged this approach by arguing that differences between the talk of men and women were 'cultural'. Men and women belonged to their own subcultures where they learnt different rules for speaking because they grew up with completely different notions of themselves, their roles and futures. Tannen was interested in what men and women were trying to 'do' in their conversations and characterised male speech as being more oriented to the world of reference as contrasted with female speech, which was more oriented to exploring and maintaining social relations. Whereas earlier research had seen many of the features of women's speech as signs of their subordination (e.g. interpreting women's more frequent use of question tags as revealing a need for 'approval' from the addressee for what they were saying), Tannen's approach reinterpreted these features according to the different aims of men and women in conversation and their different 'gender scripts'. Women speakers might use more question tags than men, not because they were automatically 'weak' speakers, but because certain uses of question tags can help to build rapport with the addressee. Similarly, Tannen's 'difference' theory avoided interpreting all male interruptions of female speech as intentionally hostile.

With its focus firmly on what was thought to distinguish female from male speech, the 'difference' approach was not particularly concerned with speech variations between members of the same sex. Yet it is obvious that there can be significant linguistic differences between same-sex speakers who, for example, belong to different social networks. A group of retired, middle-class professional men will not use English in exactly the same way as a group of young male builders. The two groups are also likely to interact with women of their own generation differently, to have a distinctive understanding of their masculinity and of how it can be enacted or 'performed' through language, as well as through social behaviour and appearance. Furthermore, even where class or ethnicity or age may be equal across several male or female individuals, sexuality may well not be. This additional dimension undermines both the 'dominance' and the 'difference' theories of gender and language, since the former cannot really account for such male speech styles as *camp*, and the latter seems to ignore the fact that some individuals might come to identify more with the subcultures formed around sexuality than those based on female and male gender norms. It is particularly in these contexts that it makes sense to talk about gender being 'performed', a concept that the next section will explore in more detail.

6.4.3 Performativity

Sexuality, like ethnicity, age, social class and other factors, can have a significant effect on how femininity and masculinity are constructed through the language. More precisely, what I am referring to here is the construction and representation of plural and diverse 'femininities' and 'masculinities' through English and not simply an opposition between heterosexuality and homosexuality. Depending on the degree of sexual freedom within a particular cultural context, the language can express a whole range of gendered identities and choices that may draw on, subvert and reconstitute notions of femaleness and maleness. For example, consider for a moment the words used in the following sample of personal ads from magazines. What kinds of femininity and masculinity do they represent?

Which words denoting gender are used 'normatively' and which are used 'subversively'?

a. Tall, dark and handsome male, likes pubs, clubs, cinema, football and nights in, seeks caring and sharing female for lasting relationship.

b. Cute, handsome, laid-back, boyish F, 25, GSOH, likes animals, pubs, cinema, etc. Seeks feminine F, GSOH, for nights in and out.

c. Sincere, conscientious, post-op F transsexual, 46, brown hair/eyes, smoker, student, into sport and community issues. WLTM caring, sharing F, 40–60, for friendship +.

d. Masculine, straight-acting/looking, submissive M, 40s, seeks dominant, firm M for fun times.[1]

In (**a**) *tall, dark and handsome* is being used in the traditional clichéd sense of heterosexual male attractiveness, so that *caring and sharing* also takes on the conventional sense of the female as nurturer and homemaker. In (**b**), by contrast, the adjectives *handsome* and *boyish* describe a lesbian, as does *feminine*, these words now subverting their normative gender meanings. In (**c**) the heterosexual norm is subverted by *post-op F transsexual*, so that the later *caring, sharing* has connotations of sensitivity and reliability in the context of a relationship in which one partner has undergone gender realignment. In (**d**) both *masculine* and *submissive* are chosen by a gay man to describe his outward appearance and his preferred sexual role respectively, thus subverting the normative connection between 'masculine' and 'dominant'. Likewise, while his ideal partner is described in terms that do not have this kind of 'contradiction' (*dominant, firm*), they too subvert the connection between maleness, dominance and heterosexuality. It is clear from these examples that sexuality is an arena in which words are used inventively and creatively to represent kinds of femininity and masculinity within gendered social networks. These networks have intersections, as implied by the term *straight-acting* (to denote gay individuals who choose to appear publicly as heterosexual), so they have a certain amount of common lexis. However, the connotations of particular words will vary according to the readership targeted. For example, the meanings of *cute* when placed next to *handsome, laid-back, boyish F* are rather different from its meanings, say, alongside *bubbly, attractive lady seeks charming gentleman*. In the former the word seems to suggest that, while the female's lesbian sexuality tends towards masculinity in terms of her appearance, she has an attractive, non-aggressive nature. In the latter, it would seem to imply that the female is 'girlish', non-feminist and likely to be attractive to men who might want to adopt a slightly paternal role towards her.

---

[1] F: female; M: Male; GSOH: good sense of humour; post-op: post-operation; WLTM: would like to meet.

6.4.4   Gay, lesbian and transgender discourses

We saw in the previous section that lexis is an important signal of gender performance in English, whether words are gender-neutralised and applied to both women and men, or whether new terms are introduced to account for gender choices for which there were previously lexical gaps. Of course, once gender-based social networks are firmly established, characteristics in their use of language can evolve that are not merely restricted to vocabulary. In the case of the gay community, this can be illustrated through the speech style known as *camp*. 'Camp', as a noun, is defined without specific reference to gender in the *New Oxford Dictionary of English* as 'deliberately exaggerated and theatrical behaviour or style: *Hollywood camp*', but the entries for *camp* as an adjective and verb refer specifically to men being ostentatiously effeminate. Camp talk can be seen as the verbal equivalent of the visual and gestural semiotic structures that distinguish drag queens from both women and other gay men and articulate their subculture. Camp, as a speech style, parodies a stereotype of femininity associated with glamour, theatricality, emotionalism and superficiality. In a study of representations of camp talk in post-1945 fiction, Harvey (2000) has described it as oriented towards particular strategies, including those he labels 'Inversion' and 'Parody'. Among the linguistic surface features of these underlying strategies, Harvey notes 'incongruities of register', 'gendered proper nouns and grammatical gender markers'; 'puns/wordplay' and 'use of French', 'exclamation' and 'vocatives'. In the fictional texts discussed by Harvey, incongruities of register can be seen in the way characters combine high or literary registers with seedy topics. He quotes this description by a character in Larry Kramer's *Faggots* (1978) of a sexual encounter in a toilet:

> He immediately inquires, 'how much?' I, not expecting such bountiful tidings, because I would have done him for free . . . I am saying 'My pleasure'.
>
> (Larry Kramer, 1978 *Faggots* London: Minerva)

Harvey notes 'a disjuncture between the topic (sex in a toilet) and the predominant register, which is formal ("inquires")', as well as 'a register hiatus within the discourse itself, with the abrupt appearance of the vulgar and unadorned "done him for free" after the apparently secure establishment of the higher register' (Harvey, 2000:244). To illustrate the use of gendered names as part of the camp strategy of 'Inversion', Harvey quotes the following passage from Quentin Crisp's autobiography *The Naked Civil Servant* (1968), in which, following arrest for soliciting, the male narrator recalls what a male friend had told him:

> A young man called Bermondsey Lizzie had once said, 'You'll get years one of these days, girl, but you'll tell them everything won't you?' – when you come up for trial, I mean. I'll never forgive you if you don't.'
>
> (Quentin Crisp, 1968 *The Naked Civil Servant* London: Cape)

Gender reversal can be seen here in the name *Lizzie* and the vocative *girl*, and, as Harvey points out, there is also a reversal of what he calls the 'expected rhetorical routines' (another surface feature of the 'Inversion' strategy) in the final clause *if you don't* (we expect this to be *if you do*). Harvey notes that the use of French words in camp English, a surface feature of the parodic strategy, has possible origins in the historical opposition of aristocratic and middle-class models of selfhood, but that the use of French words is not confined to the representation of aristocratic homosexuals. With regard to exclamations and vocatives, Harvey writes that the two frequently combine in camp talk to create a 'verbal style that is addressee-oriented and gossipy' (Harvey, 2000:255).

Although Harvey's article focuses mainly on the fictional representations of camp talk and not the naturally occurring speech of homosexual subcultures, fictional camp discourse is often written by authors who are themselves part of, or familiar with, gay social networks and how English is used within them. Also, non-fictional observations (for example, on the letters pages of gay magazines) tend to support the view that the speech styles of some homosexual subcultures, or even of the 'scene' more generally, are sometimes characterised by theatrical and ostentatious linguistic effects built up around stereotypes of femininity.

How far is it also possible to identify a distinctive speech style for 'butch' or masculine-oriented lesbian identities? When contemporary female comics perform sketches about butch lesbians, their speech styles tend to parody 'macho' male speech (which typically might involve the use of taboo or sexist terms and non-cooperative conversational strategies), but it is hard to tell whether this is a discourse that would prove to be as distinctive as camp if studied systematically from a sociolinguistic perspective. This is perhaps due to the fact that camp is more than just a speech style – it is also a kind of debunking and deconstructive attitude to life – whereas 'butch' does not appear to have this scope. However, the evidence from advertisements in personal columns, magazines, websites and fiction all points to different lesbian identities being linguistically distinguishable at least on the lexical level. And, interestingly, where closed group interaction between lesbians has been represented fictionally, discourse strategies similar to those noted by Harvey in camp talk can be discovered. The following passage is taken from a novel published in 1998 about the adventures of the young lesbian narrator in London in the 1890s. Here she is being accompanied for the first time by her older and richer lover, Diana, to a secret lesbian club near Piccadilly:

> We walked through a hush that was thick as bristling velvet – for, at our appearance at the door the lady members had turned their heads to stare, and then had goggled. Whether, like Miss Hawkins, they took me for a gentleman; or whether – like Diana – they had seen through my disguise at once, I cannot say. Either way, there was a cry – 'Good gracious!' – and then another

exclamation, more lingering: 'My *word* . . .' I felt Diana stiffen at my side, with pure complacency.

Then came another shout, as a lady at a table in the farthest corner rose to her feet. 'Diana, you old roué! You have done it at last!' She gave a clap. Beside her, two more ladies looked on, pink-faced. One of them had a monocle, and now she fixed it to her eye.

Diana placed me before them all, and presented me – more graciously than she had introduced me to Miss Hawkins, but again as her 'companion'; and the ladies laughed. The first of them, the one who had risen to greet us, now seized my hand. Her fingers held a stubby cigar.

'This, Nancy dear,' said my mistress, 'is Mrs Jex. She is quite my oldest friend in London – and quite the most disreputable. Everything she tells you will be designed to corrupt.'

I bowed to her. I said, 'I hope so, indeed.' Mrs Jex gave a roar.

'But it speaks!' she cried. 'All this' – she gestured to my face, my costume – 'and the creature even speaks!'

(Sarah Waters, 1998 *Tipping the Velvet* London: Virago Press)

Like camp talk, the speech represented here also uses strategies of inversion, particularly with regard to expected rhetorical routines. When Diana announces that Mrs Jex is 'quite the most disreputable' of her friends, she inverts the usual introductory norms of attributing 'good' rather than 'bad' characteristics to one's friends. The narrator then also inverts the expected reply by saying 'I hope so, indeed', rather than expressing disbelief, shock or fear. Here there is also, of course, a shared double-entendre, with 'disreputable' carrying the coded meaning of being unbound by sexual convention. Similarly, the word 'companion' produces a laugh, as it is code here for lesbian lover. As in Harvey's description of camp talk, mimicry of an aristocracy free of moral control is also suggested by the use of a borrowed French term in 'you old roué', though here it is masculinity that is parodied through the loud and insinuating exclamations of some of the women, as well as the impolite language used by Mrs Jex at the end of the extract when she refers to the narrator as 'it' and 'the creature'. Such language also contrasts with the narrator's own polite, or 'mock polite', terms in alluding to the 'lady members' and to the fact that she was taken by Miss Hawkins 'for a gentleman'.

The fictional representations of gay and lesbian subcultures in this section show that sexuality is actively constructed and 'performed' through language. This is particularly the case where speakers are socialising informally and generating shared inferences for their own entertainment.

6.5 Gender in social discourse

The linguistic blurring of gender boundaries is by no means restricted to gay, lesbian and transgender subcultures or fictional writing about them. Domains such as the fashion industry also challenge the norms of femininity and masculinity in order to target and attract particular consumers. Fashion designers and those who write about fashion both reflect a pluralistically gendered society and encourage even more diversity and instability within it. The following commentary on new trends in designer menswear exploits both normative and diversified masculinity to the full:

> Sorry guys, but if you anticipate that a 34-inch waist will suffice for next summer's wardrobe, it's time you registered at Weight Watchers. While the anorexia argument has become fashion's equivalent of an old chestnut on the womenswear circuit, the same debate may well raise its weary head in the aftermath of the menswear collections; designers in Milan and Paris rejected pumped pectorals and rippling abdomens for a leaner, more lithe silhouette, as narrow as a knife blade and just as uncompromising.
>
> Assuming that you have the perfect torso, further sartorial decisions lie ahead, mostly dependent on how in touch you are with your feminine side. If you can't fight the lure of bubblegum-pink leather jackets and stretch-lace shirts, then Versace and Dolce & Gabbana will make the perfect talking point at your next men's-group meeting. Whereas if you're the macho motorbike-racing type, it's Louis Vuitton that will whisk you into the sunset on the back of a Harley Davidson. Butch vs camp may well be understandable in light of the fact that a sizeable proportion of designer menswear is geared towards the pink-pound customer.
>
> (Andrew Tucker, 'Return of the thin man', *The Times*,
> Part 2, 9 July 2001)

This text relies to a great extent on shared social knowledge for its effects. We need to know that 'Weight Watchers' is an organisation that helps people to lose weight; that 'the anorexia argument' refers to the claims of some commentators that many female fashion models in recent times have been so thin that they seem undernourished and could even be suffering from eating disorders such as anorexia; and that the 'pink-pound customer' is the stereotypical gay customer, often assumed to be a professional with a large disposable income.

The text appears to be just as much about alternative masculinities as about new fashion and its implied readership is consequently diverse. 'Sorry guys' seems to appeal to the 'ordinary' male who might not normally care too much about his waistline but whose attitude may now have to change. The qualification 'dependent on how in touch you are with your feminine side' presupposes that the male reader understands that a 'modern' man may wish to acknowledge and develop the feminine side of his nature. While the reference to the 'next men's-group meeting' takes this a step further, with men being represented in caring and sharing roles, 'macho motorbike-racing type' returns us abruptly to the construction of the male as an independent, competitive adventurer, an image rather romantically reinforced by 'whisk you into the sunset on the back of a Harley Davidson'. The text seems to say there is something for every kind of man in the latest designer menswear, since there is no male image or lifestyle that today's fashion world has not taken into account. Texts like this one represent a kind of educated, liberal social discourse – in this case found within the 'Culture' section of a quality British newspaper. Such discourses tend both to influence mainstream attitudes towards gender and to reflect how far the mainstream has already absorbed what might previously have been regarded as offbeat or subversive.

6.6 Summary

In this chapter we have considered gender from the perspective of the English language itself, as well as from the perspectives of talk, sexuality and social discourse. We have seen that, while some of the imbalances in the representation of females and males have been neutralised in the language, others remain, and stereotypical views of how women and men converse are still common. However, linguists and gender theorists have moved towards seeing gender in terms of performativity rather than through traditional oppositions, an approach which is proving better able to describe, and account for, the many diverse ways in which gender is represented in English today.

Activities

1. Compare a set of advertisements for skincare products, some designed for women and some for men. Is it possible to guess the gender of the target customer from the way the product is described? If you find some products targeted at both women and men, consider how the descriptions of these differ from the other advertisements.

2. Record and transcribe part of a TV or radio discussion between 'experts' of both sexes (e.g. a contemporary arts review). Given that the status of all the participants is assumed to be equal, are the speaking turns fairly evenly balanced between the female and male speakers, or do the male speakers (as research has suggested) actually talk more than the females? Does the gender of the person chairing the discussion have a bearing on this? Do the women use more hedges and modals like 'may', 'could', 'really', 'perhaps'? Do the men interrupt the women more than the other way round? Do any speakers talk in ways that contest their normative gender roles? If so, how do they do this and how do the others react?

3. Analyse two or three examples of writing with marked gender connotations. One approach, for example, could be to compare a dialogue between a traditional hero and heroine from romantic fiction and a fictional dialogue between gay or lesbian partners. Explore the texts from the point of view of their lexis, grammar and any descriptions or indications of the characters' speech styles.

Further Reading

For a clear and well-illustrated introduction to sexism in English and to gendered talk see Thomas and Wareing (1999). Coates (1996) and Coates and Cameron (1988) are useful references for studies of all-female conversation. Cameron (1998) has extensive coverage of feminist studies of gender and language, analysing both sexist discourse and gender performativity. See Eckert and McConnell-Ginet (2003) for a more recent introduction to the study of language and gender. For more on theories of sexuality and of sexuality and language see Bristow (1997) and Cameron and Kulick (2003).

Chapter 7

Speech, Writing and the New Media

7.1 Introduction

Most introductory texts in sociolinguistics cover the topic of speech and writing, outlining the differences between these modes of communication. However, although this is therefore quite a familiar subject, it is now becoming a more complex one, because speech and writing are not quite as clearly distinguishable in some contexts of English use as they once were. Technological advances have to some degree broken down the traditional choice between talking and writing, so that millions of us today, especially younger people, spend time communicating through new channels, particularly email, mobile phone and online discussion forums. In this chapter, we will consider not only some of the established differences between speech and writing, and issues concerning the study of these modes, but also the varieties of English evolving through computer-mediated or 'electronic' communication.

7.2 Spontaneous speech

Speech is spontaneous when we are talking naturally and informally, for example with friends and colleagues, and it is characterised mostly by its non-rehearsed or non-prepared nature. Along with our interlocutor, we have no plan of where the conversation will go and how it will work out. Of course, authentic informal talk is often a lot more than just empty 'small talk', and so we probably do have, for much of the time, certain expectations as to where such talk is leading and what, for instance, we would like to talk about. If I bump into a colleague with whom I have recently made some practical arrangement, it is highly probable that this will be referred to in our talk, even if only in passing. In other words, conversation is not strictly unplanned in the sense that the interlocutors have absolutely no conscious aims in the talk whatsoever, but only in the sense that, *linguistically*, they have not already worked out what forms of the language they are going to use to express what they want to say. In their heads, they may well have quite clear intentions, but they will actually express these intentions spontaneously, if and when they get the chance to in the course of the conversation.

Although informal conversation does not appear to be closely controlled in any way, it does have its own tacit set of rules relating to how we open and close talk; how we greet each other; how we give listener feedback or **back-channel support** by saying *yes, exactly, mhm*, etc.; how we ask and answer questions, make and respond to suggestions, and so on. Sometimes what we say is partly ritualised or formulaic, so that one person's utterance will tend to trigger a fairly automatic response. Utterances such as *I'm sorry* followed by *It's OK* are examples of such sequences and are called **adjacency pairs**. Speakers adept at holding the floor tend to avoid pausing at the end of a sentence (a predictable 'completion point'). Instead they tend to pause when the sentence is still incomplete and it is harder for others to intervene. When speakers are ready to yield the floor, however, they may look at their interactants more steadily, particularly at the person they think is going to speak next. To signal that they want to take a turn, that person may show some physical tension, lean forward slightly and audibly draw in breath. Of course, it is also possible for speakers to make this wish explicit, as they do when they say *Look, you're not letting me get a word in*. The verbal cues meaning 'I demand my turn' can, however, be considered impolite, which is why they are found more frequently in conversations between people who know one another well, such as friends and members of the same family.

Authentic talk reveals the fact that it is spontaneously formulated in various noticeable ways, mainly by the presence of **non-fluency features** such as the following:

- Abandoned/incomplete words such as *thi-this* and abandoned and/or reformulated sentence structure, such as *I could always get the tickets from . . . there's a new box office down . . . you know, when you go through that new shopping arcade . . .*
- Syntactic blends, where the structure of a sentence changes 'in mid-stream', e.g. *About two hundred years ago we had ninety-five per cent of people in this country were employed in farming.*
- Mispronunciations and slips of the tongue, e.g. *par cark* for *car park* (syllable-onset consonants swopped); *win a pin* for *with a pin* (where an anticipated consonant is articulated early).
- Fillers like *er, erm*.
- Repetition (often combined with hesitation), such as *it's . . . it's . . . n . . . not that I want to be critical but . . .*

7.3 Transcribing speech

When transcribing speech, especially conversation, analysts usually decide to use a set of notational conventions to represent intonation and other features (such as pauses or overlapping speech), though the level of detail will depend on the purpose of the transcription and the number of features being studied. No single or universal set of conventions exists for the transcription of speech, but most systems combine IPA and keyboard symbols. Unless there is a special interest in the accents of the speakers, a non-phonetic transcription is used. Note that normal use of capitals, commas and full stops is not generally found in transcriptions of speech, though proper nouns retain their initial capitals and apostrophes are kept for contracted forms and possessive constructions. It is acceptable to be selective in our choice of conventions as long as we provide a key and apply the symbols consistently and clearly.

The following conventions are quite commonly adopted for studying the general features of conversational interaction:

→	utterance continues without a break to next arrow
←	utterance continued from last arrow
=	smooth 'latching' (no break between speaking turns)
?	intonation indicates a question (whether or not grammatical form is interrogative)
↑	marked rise in pitch begins here
↓	marked lowering in pitch begins here
italics	marked emphasis on word
CAPITALS	indicates shouting
(xxx)	indecipherable text
(word)	indicates uncertainty that this word was used
((frowns))	non-verbal behaviour, e.g. frowning
(.)	a micropause (not measurable)
(3.2)	pause measured in seconds
[	start of overlapping speech
]	end of overlapping speech
°word(s)°	word(s) said quietly
hhh-	breathing out very audibly
.hhh	breathing in very audibly
: : :	elongated word or syllable (e.g. it was ama: : :zing)

Transcribing a stretch of informal conversation reveals interesting aspects of the grammar of speech. One of the most important features is the tendency for speakers to omit parts of grammatical structures where they are easily understood from the context. Take this short exchange:

A: coming to lunch?
B: sorry (.) too busy

In A's question, both the auxiliary 'are' and the subject 'you' are left out, since the addressee is clear from the context and the rising intonation indicates the intended question. Similarly, B omits 'I'm' twice in the reply, because it is understood that no one else is being referred to. This type of structural ellipsis can also occur in informal writing (e.g. messages between friends) but it is a very common feature of conversation. It is not restricted to conversational speech genres, however. In some other spoken varieties, such as sports commentary, it can be even more marked. Listen to any live commentary of a sport involving quick sequences of action by different players and you will almost certainly find that ellipsis is very noticeable. A football commentator on radio might say *over to Beckham* (.) *looking for Owen* (.) *passes to Owen* (.) *Owen sees a gap*, leaving out everything but the most essential information that the listener needs, namely which player has the ball and what he is doing with it.

When authentic conversation is recorded in writing, for purposes of study, research or official record-keeping, we need to be aware that certain features of the original conversation are almost bound to have been left out. Even a detailed phonetic transcription, aiming to capture every peculiarity of an individual's pronunciation, cannot on its own give us the 'quality' of their actual voice in the way an audio recording can. As we have seen, speech can be transcribed by linguists for a variety of different purposes, which inevitably entails a selective approach to the features to be described. When speech is transcribed for non-academic purposes, however, such as to record the proceedings of parliament, the result is often not the completely accurate account expected, but a tidied-up version which, for example, filters out non-fluency features such as incomplete utterances and repetitions thought unnecessary, or changes the level of formality by giving the full versions of contracted forms. Here is an example of how an institutionalised method of transcription (in this case, of British parliamentary debates) differs from one using linguistically motivated conventions:

(a) . but that . Mr Deputy Speaker . I hasten to stress . is the aspirations of . Tory politicians looking . to the election . rather than the aspirations of the British people . I I I think looking to a Government . that actually is prepared to face up to the problems . which according to all the indicators the British people feel . the Government ought to face up to . and I can only say Mr Deputy Speaker . that this is a Budget for deepening the inequalities . that have been aggravated . by eight years of Conservative rule .

(b) Those are the aspirations of Tory politicians looking to the election, not the aspirations of the British people looking to a Government who are prepared to face the problems which, according to all the indicators, they feel the Government ought to face up to. This Budget deepens the inequalities that have been aggravated by eight years of Conservative rule.

(Stef Slembrouck, 1992)

In addition to its tidying up of the grammar in (a), changing *that . . . is the aspirations* to *Those are the aspirations*, and omitting the hesitation in *I I I think*, the officially recorded version in (b) in fact omits many of the ways in which the member of Parliament speaking actually presented his point of view. The interpersonal and textual dimensions of the speech, as revealed by *I hasten to stress* or *actually* or *I can only say Mr Deputy Speaker*, are clearly reduced to favour the ideational dimension, or the concepts being communicated. Also, there is a subtle distortion of meaning in changing *this is a Budget for deepening the inequalities*, with its implication that the Government introduced it in almost wilful indifference to the social consequences, to *This Budget deepens the inequalities*, which represents the utterance as a factual claim.

7.4 Rehearsed speech

Rehearsed speech is speech that is in some way prepared and/or practised before it is delivered or recorded for later transmission. Although the aim might well be to sound spontaneous and natural, rehearsed speech doesn't just 'happen' in the way everyday conversations do and so it cannot be truly spontaneous. Nevertheless, it can have *some* of the characteristics of spontaneous speech. If a speaker is delivering a prepared speech but not actually reading it aloud from a complete script, there will be opportunities for the occurrence of non-fluency features like syntactic blends, fillers and hesitation markers.

When Tony Blair became Prime Minister of Britain in 1997, one of his first duties was to deliver, in accordance with tradition, a speech outside 10 Downing Street, thanking the electorate and summarising the aims of the government he was about to form. Although the speech was not read aloud, it was evident that its sequence and content had been carefully prepared. At the same time, however, this was a moment of some elation and excitement for Mr Blair, so that keeping faithfully to a rehearsed speech must have been quite difficult. As you read the following extract from a transcribed version of the speech, consider which aspects are characteristic of rehearsed speech and which are more spontaneous:

Thank you very much indeed. I shall say to you that I have just accepted Her Majesty the Queen's kind offer to form a new administration of government in this country.
I should like to begin if I may by paying tribute to my predecessor John Major for his dignity and his courage over these last few days and for the manner of his leaving, the essential decency of which is the mark of the man and I am pleased to pay tribute to him.

As I stand here before No 10 Downing Street, I know all too well the huge responsibility that is upon me and the great trust that the British people have placed in me.

I know well what this country has voted for today. It is a mandate for New Labour and I say to the people of this country . . . we ran for office as New Labour, we will govern as New Labour.

This is not a mandate for dogma or for doctrine, or a return to the past, but it was a mandate to get those things done in our country that desperately need doing for the future of Britain. . . .

(Printed in *The Times*, 3 May 1997)

You will probably feel, as I do, that this extract is characterised mostly by a dignified tone, if not a degree of gravitas, since Blair is acknowledging the national importance of the moment and appealing to the concept of national unity (*the British people; our country; future of Britain*). Yet he gets off to a slightly awkward start with the rather stilted *I shall say to you* (*shall* is a rare form in spontaneous speech today), perhaps because he is more concerned at this point to ensure a sufficiently 'correct' and gracious reference to the Queen (*Her Majesty the Queen's kind offer*). Indeed, this is a highly conventionalised reference, as it is the people who have actually elected Blair and made it possible for him to lead the new government, and not the Queen, as he emphasises later. The next section, in which he refers to John Major, the outgoing Prime Minister, is also quite formal and/or formulaic in its vocabulary (*paying tribute; dignity and courage*) as well as in aspects of its grammar (*if I may*) but there are also more relaxed features, such as the general phrase *over these last few days*, the idiomatic *the mark of the man*, and the use of coordination with *and* in *and I am pleased to pay tribute to him*, where Blair is reinforcing, in the way we do in conversation, the point he is making. This simple coordinated structure contrasts with the formality of what precedes it (*for the manner of his leaving, the essential decency of which is the mark of the man*) and is likely to have been formulated spontaneously. On the other hand, nominalisations such as *the manner of his leaving* are very atypical of spontaneous speech, yet they also serve the purpose of referring more politely to Major's defeat than *the way he is leaving* would. Blair now goes on to refer to the responsibility he is to carry, and again we find an emphasis on rhetorical formality: the mention in full of *No 10 Downing Street* when the TV pictures show Blair standing directly in front of the building stresses the symbolic importance of the context; similarly, *responsibility that is upon me* and *great trust that the British people have placed in me* belong to the stock expressions used by generations of British Prime Ministers. The rest of the extract gives us ample evidence of the rehearsed aspects of Blair's speech with the carefully controlled *we ran for office as New Labour, we will govern as New Labour*, yet there is an unnecessary and probably accidental change of tense in *This is not a mandate . . . , but it was a mandate*, the sort of inadvertent adjustment that speakers make when they simply forget which tense it was that they started out with. Overall, what a speech of this kind shows is that, even at the most nationally significant moments, public figures do not wholly abandon the instincts of the spontaneous speaker. Indeed, their intention, in most cases today, is to sound natural and confident in their delivery rather than artificially flawless. However, there is sometimes a thin dividing line between sounding confidently natural and being vulnerable to the less welcome mishaps of spontaneous speech, such as total breakdowns in structure or inconsistency in the orientational features of language (e.g. tense, pronoun use). The Blair extract is rehearsed but not wholly memorised speech and therefore, as we have seen, remains vulnerable in places to some of the difficulties of on-the-spot formulation.

Another kind of rehearsed speech, though, *is* usually memorised: this is speech in drama. Here, of course, there are important differences in the relationship between the speaker and the content of the speech. Politicians and teachers are purportedly committed to the truth of what they say, while actors are not. Plays also vary in the extent to which they set out to imitate the features of spontaneous speech. While some stylised sub-genres avoid naturalistic speech altogether, other genres aim for as much 'authenticity' as possible. However, the vast majority of plays fall somewhere between these two extremes, attempting to represent the speech of their characters realistically enough for us to be able to believe in them. Let us turn for a moment to an extract from a well-known play in this naturalistic tradition and consider how it represents a conversation between a father and his sons:

WILLY: I'm not interested in stories about the past or any crap of that kind because the woods are burning, boys, you understand? There's a big blaze going on all around. I was fired today.
BIFF [*shocked*]: How could you be?
WILLY: I was fired, and I'm looking for a little good news to tell your mother, because the woman has waited and the woman has suffered. The gist of it is that I haven't got a story left in my head, Biff. So don't give me a lecture about facts and aspects. I am not interested. Now what've you got to say to me?
[*Stanley enters with three drinks. They wait until he leaves.*]
WILLY: Did you see Oliver?
BIFF: Jesus, Dad!
WILLY: You mean you didn't go up there?
HAPPY: Sure he went up there.
BIFF: I did. I – saw him. How could they fire you?
WILLY [*on the edge of his chair*]: What kind of a welcome did he give you?
BIFF: He won't even let you work on commission?
WILLY: I'm out! [*Driving*] So tell me, he gave you a warm welcome?
HAPPY: Sure, Pop, sure!

BIFF [*driven*]: Well, it was kind of –

WILLY: I was wondering if he'd remember you. [*To Happy*] Imagine, man doesn't see him for ten, twelve years and gives him that kind of a welcome!

HAPPY: Damn right!

BIFF [*trying to return to the offensive*]: Pop, look –

WILLY: You know why he remembered you, don't you? Because you impressed him in those days.

BIFF: Let's talk quietly and get this down to the facts, huh?

WILLY [*as though Biff had been interrupting*]: Well, what happened? It's great news, Biff. Did he take you into his office or'd you talk in the waiting-room?

BIFF: Well, he came in, see, and –

WILLY [*with a big smile*]: What'd he say? Betcha he threw his arm around you.

BIFF: Well, he kinda –

WILLY: He's a fine man. [*To Happy*] Very hard man to see, y'know.

HAPPY [*agreeing*]: Oh, I know.

WILLY [*to Biff*]: Is that where you had the drinks?

BIFF: Yeah, he gave me a couple of – no, no!

HAPPY [*cutting in*]: He told him my Florida idea.

WILLY: Don't interrupt. [*To Biff*] How'd he react to the Florida idea?

BIFF: Dad, will you give me a minute to explain?

WILLY: I've been waiting for you to explain since I sat down here! What happened? He took you into his office and what?

BIFF: Well – I talked. And – and he listened, see.

WILLY: Famous for the way he listens, y'know. What was his answer?

BIFF: His answer was – [*He breaks off, suddenly angry.*] Dad, you're not letting me tell you what I want to tell you!

(Arthur Miller, 1949 *Death of a Salesman* London: Methuen)

This extract has many of the features of spontaneous conversation, such as speakers trying to hold on to their turns or to interrupt another speaker, which in some cases are reinforced by stage directions such as [*Driving*] or [*cutting in*]. There are also general fillers like *Well, it was kind of* and *Well, he kinda* –, and grammatical ellipses are shown in *Betcha* (for *I'll bet you*) and *man doesn't see him for ten, twelve years* . . . (omitting *the* before *man*). Non-standard spelling is used to represent realistic features of informal pronunciation such as assimilation (*Betcha*), reduced vowels (*y'know*) and elision (*or'd* for *or did*). The speakers also check that they're being listened to in ways characteristic of ordinary talk, using *y'know* and *see*. Most noticeable of all, however, is the way in which they sometimes skip back to earlier turns, as when Biff asks *How could they fire you?* several turns after Will has announced his dismissal and attempted to change the subject, asking about the visit to Oliver. This kind of manoeuvring is frequently found in conversations, especially those involving more than two people. Finally, there are the verbalised appeals for greater cooperation which can often be found in family conversations, as when Biff demands *Dad, will you give me a minute to explain?* Overall, then, we have in this extract a representation of how close drama can come to sounding like spontaneous speech. The important thing to remember, though, is that dramatic speech only does come this close to ordinary talk when it is appropriate to the techniques and aims of the play as a whole – in this case, it needs to do so, because the tragic story of the unsuccessful salesman Willy Loman is intended to be credible and emotionally compelling to the audience.

7.5 Written English

Although some of the speech we have looked at so far was written to be spoken, as in the extract from *Death of a Salesman*, our focus in this section will now move to variation within written English and how the conventions of writing can be exploited to serve different communicative purposes. First, however, we will consider briefly attitudes towards the spelling of English.

7.5.1 Spelling

As we saw in Chapter 3, the spelling of English did not become fully standardised until the great lexicographers Samuel Johnson (for British English) and Noah Webster (for American English) attempted to promote the use of 'correct' orthographic forms, although there had been attempts to standardise and reform spelling as early as the 16th and 17th centuries. Johnson was influenced mainly by etymology and usage, though Webster was a reformer guided partially by phonographic considerations, advocating a closer link between the sounds and written symbols of the language. The American English spelling of words like *center, honor* and *defense* (rather than *centre, honour* and *defence*) goes back to choices made by Webster, showing his preference for omitting superfluous and indeterminate letters. Some later reformers, including the US statesmen Benjamin Franklin and Theodore Roosevelt, the publisher and educational reformer Isaac Pitman, the linguists Henry Sweet and Daniel Jones, and the dramatist George Bernard Shaw, experimented with amended or new English alphabets or supported societies aiming to reform spelling, yet they had no lasting influence on the written language. The anomalies of English spelling are well documented and a notorious source of difficulty for learners of the language in all parts of the world, yet even reformers generally believe that gradual simplification is better than an attempt to introduce radical change.

Ironically, perhaps, the very internationalism of English today makes re-forming its spelling difficult, since it would be hard to achieve a consensus on new spellings, and phonographic reform would entail the politically sensitive task of choosing a specific accent of English on which to base the new orthography, which in many parts of the world would be seen as a political, not merely linguistic, choice. Another problem for the reformers has been the fact that people tend to be quite conservative in their attitude to orthography and to react negatively to the appearance of radically altered spelling, often seeing it as 'ugly' or analogous to semi-literacy. Issues about spelling still provoke a great deal of public anxiety, as was seen recently when it was announced that schoolchildren in Britain would be expected to use internationally agreed spellings for scientific terms like *fetus* (instead of *foetus*). The public outcry was such that the British government immedi-ately acted to reassure parents that this would not be the case after all and that schoolchildren would be allowed to continue using British spellings for scientific nomenclature. A few extracts from the contributions to an Internet chatline hosted by the *Sun* tabloid on the subject of using American spelling will provide an overview of how this debate about a specific area of spell-ing quickly fuelled the flames of the traditional linguistic and cultural rivalry between Britain and the US:

1. As the language is ours the world should adopt our spelling and to hell with the arrogance of the USA.
2. As a Canadian, I think that this is horrible! The English language should be left just that – British. We cannot allow the Americans to wipe out a cultural identity. From my earliest years, I have been taught to use British spelling, so lets keep that tradition alive.
3. Sheesh! What's wrong with you Brits? It is an international agreement. There-fore, compromise was used to determine which words and phrases needed to be uniform [so] as to not cause confusion and chaos in science, suppos-edly, an exact medium. It was certainly not designed to dictate 'American English' as the only correct spelling. Just to make sure that everyone used the same vernacular to avoid serious errors. Why they don't just use Latin is beyond me. Grow up Brits and stop your petty whining.

('Should we use American spellings?', *The Sun Newspaper Online*, 24 November 2000. Website: http://www.the-sun.co.uk/)

In spite of the strong feelings that spelling seems to be able to provoke, written English is surprisingly uniform across the world. The well-known differences between American and British English spelling illustrated by words such as *jeweler/jeweller; traveled/travelled; apologize/apologise; esthetic/aesthetic; catalog/catalogue; skeptical/sceptical* (the normal American spelling is the first in each pair) do not amount to major differences in what we see on the page and do not seriously affect our ability to read the language. Indeed, pronunciation differences between English dialects can be far more of a barrier to understanding.

Despite the general uniformity of English spelling, however, some uses and varieties of the language allow for considerable experimentalism and flexibility. Read through the following examples taken from two different written texts and consider how and why the spelling conventions of Standard English have not been followed:

a) Finaly, ze unesesary 'o' kuld be dropd from vords kontaining 'ou'. Similar arguments vud of kors be aplid to ozer konbinations of leters. Kontinuing zis proses yer aftr yer, ve vud eventuli hav a reli sensibl riten stil. Aftr twenti yers zer vud be no mor trubls or difikultis and evrion vud fin it ezi tu understan esh ozer. Ze drems of ze E.U. vud finali kum tru.

(Emily Sheffield, 'Easy speak: Changes to the English Language in the European Union', copyright Guardian Newspapers Limited 1996)

b) Elizabeth Bates rose. Rigley was a big man, with very large bones. His head looked particularly bony. Across his temple was a blue scar, caused by a wound got in the pit, a wound in which the coal-dust remained blue like tattooing.

''Asna 'e come whoam yit?' asked the man, without any form of greeting, but with deference and sympathy. 'I couldna say wheer he is – 'e's non ower theer!' – he jerked his head to signify the 'Prince of Wales.'

''E's 'appen gone up to th' "Yew,"' said Mrs. Rigley.

There was another pause. Rigley had evidently something to get off his mind. . . .

(D.H. Lawrence, 'Odour of Chrysanthemums' in James Wood, ed. 1999 *Selected Short Stories of D.H. Lawrence* New York: Random House)

These examples show some of the reasons why spelling can be deliberately altered. In **(a)** it is distorted almost beyond recognition for satirical purposes, since the writer is clearly of the persuasion that spelling reform is, as it were, the thin end of the wedge and just another dimension of the impersonal centralising tendencies at work in the way society is organised. In this case, the butt of the joke is the European Union, which is represented as pursuing apparently logical but ultimately dangerous ideals that will complicate, not simplify, people's lives. Text **(b)** describes the growing anxiety of Elizabeth Bates when her husband, a coalminer, fails to come home from work. In this extract she has swallowed her pride and decided to go and ask her neighbours if they know where he is. The spelling is non-standard only when the speech of Mr and Mrs Rigley is being represented (the 'voice' of the narrator is in Standard English). When Rigley asks '*Asna 'e come whoam yit?* ('Hasn't he come home yet?'), it reflects features of his regional and social dialect as a miner from Nottinghamshire in England, such as the lack of aspiration in *hasn't* and *he*, the changed diphthong in *home* and the different vowel in *yet*, along with the dropped final 't' in *hasn't*. The spelling reveals some features quite consistently, such as '*Asna* and *couldna, wheer* and *theer*, and lexical features of the dialect are also represented, as in '*appen* (meaning 'possibly') and *non* (meaning 'not'). To some extent, writers like Lawrence have older dialect literature to take as models or precedents, but the spellings chosen in literature to represent many regional dialects are often inconsistent and dependent more on the preferences of the individual writer than on established conventions.[2] In cases where a writer wishes to represent the idiosyncrasies of a particular character's pronunciation that are not features of group but of *idiolect* or individual variation (e.g. articulatory characteristics like lisping), they have to invent appropriate spellings accordingly.

The question 'What is written English?' may seem a very straightforward one, but in fact, the more you study different written varieties of the language, the more aware you will become of the impossibility of describing writing as a wholly separate medium from speech. Some writing is written to be spoken, other writing is written to be read. Some is for personal reference, like diaries and the lists we write for ourselves when we go shopping or the notes we make to aid our studies. Some is public, like signs, notices and posters. Then there are instruction booklets, cartoon jokes, forms, questionnaires, invoices, the minutes of meetings, legal contracts, horoscopes and reviews – the list is endless. In each case, studying varieties of written English involves looking not just at the features of the language itself but also drawing on what we know about the context in which the variety occurs and its function. Like speech, writing is a communicative act, even if we are only communicating with ourselves, and therefore we need ways of looking at 'context' just as we need ways of describing formal linguistic features. This is something which we will consider closely in the next chapter, but first we will look at an area in which writing has become a lot more like speech and where it can be said, on some occasions, to have taken the place of speech and even to have altered interpersonal communication fundamentally.

7.6 Email and text-messaging

The Internet and mobile phone technology are playing an ever-increasing role in people's daily lives, in the workplace and in educational contexts. What we might call 'electronic English' now occupies a place alongside 'spoken English' and 'written English' as a powerful new medium with its own varieties and sub-varieties.

One of the fundamental ways in which emails differ from traditional written letters is in the extent of their variability. The writer of an email can add to it, make revisions to it, delete parts of it, etc. without this editing

[2] There are, however, some exceptions to this, such as the literary variety of Scots known as Lallans (from Scots *lawlands* or lowlands) adopted after the Second World War by writers of the Scottish Renaissance movement. Lallans systematically draws many of its word forms and spellings from an archaic variety of Central Scots, retaining items such as *descryve* ('describe'), *lift* ('sky'), *aiblins* ('perhaps') and *virr* ('strength').

process leaving its mark, literally, on the text itself. On the other hand, unlike written letters, emails can sometimes lose their formatting in transmission and not look to the recipient exactly as they do on the sender's screen before being sent. Emails also have very different stylistic features from traditional letters, for example, their greater use of bullet points, tendency towards light punctuation (including possible consistent lack of capitalisation), misspellings and typing errors. They can also contain *smileys* or *emoticons*, combinations of keyboard characters (most read sideways) representing basic emotions and reactions, for example:

smiling	:-)
frowning	:-(
laughing	:-D
shocked	:-o
crying	:'-(
winking	;-)
hugging	{ }
kissing	:*
I say nothing	:-x

Of course, email style varies considerably according to the context and purpose of the communication. It would be somewhat inappropriate, for example, if applicants for an academic post were sent the following email asking them to attend an interview:

hi folks! can you please come for interview on tuesday 3 june at 10am in the school of ed. just ask for jo from app. linguistics when you get here .we look forward to meeting you then.
rgds,
trish (personnel) :-)

On the other hand, in less formal emailing contexts, most people are tolerant to a certain extent of features such as abbreviations and acronyms (as long as they're recognised), occasional typing errors like reversed or omitted letters (e.g.*aslo* instead of also; *rturn* for *return*) and use of lower case where upper case would be expected in writing (e.g. *charles wilson building* for *Charles Wilson Building*). The more such features predominate in a message, however, the less acceptable they may be to particular recipients, as they may give an impression of undue haste and carelessness on the part of the sender or even indifference to the content of the message.

The English of mobile phone text-messaging, or *texting*, is affected in a number of ways by the limited space available for the message and the usual importance of speed in both composing and replying to messages. First of all, certain letters are often used to stand in for whole words, such as *CU* and *RU* for *See you* and *Are you*, and numerals used to shorten the text, as in *B4* for *Before* and *Gr8* for *Great*. In fact, writers of text messages quickly become adept at reducing every word to its minimum comprehensible length, usually omitting vowels wherever possible, as in *Wknd* for *Weekend*, *Msg* for *Message*, or deliberately using shorter misspellings, such as *Wot* for *What*. The spaces between words are also sometimes done away with in a text message, with word boundaries shown by upper-case letters, as in *ThxForYrMsg* (*Thanks for your message*). However, ensuring clarity can be difficult if this strategy is combined, for example, with acronyms such as *AFAIK* (*As far as I know*) or *IYSWIM* (*If you see what I mean*), with the result that most messages are inconsistent in style, abbreviating some words but not others and not necessarily omitting vowels or punctuation. Nevertheless, a gimmicky text-messaging style is encouraged by the mobile phone networks themselves and some of them even supply ready-made messages (Christmas cards, love poems, etc.) illustrating this, as in *SHLL I CMPRE THEE 2 A SMMRS DAY?*, a texting version of the opening line of Shakespeare's famous 18th sonnet, *Shall I compare thee to a summer's day?*

7.7 Chat rooms and message boards

As the name suggests, a chat room is a location for online 'conversation'. Some internet chat is *synchronous* or occurs in real time – in other words messages are typed 'live' and responses are given in seconds. As in text-messaging, speed is of the essence in chat rooms, which has an effect on the forms and style of the language used. Abbreviations and acronyms are widely adopted, and it is common for a newcomer or *newbie* to be asked *a/s/l?* (querying *age/sex/location*) during the initial exchanges. While some chat rooms are dedicated to specific topics of interest, most serve the purposes of online banter and are very popular with teenagers. Since communication is text-based only, participants feel less governed by the normal conventions of spoken exchanges and may sometimes be more confrontational than they would be in face-to-face talk. However, chat rooms have 'house rules' designed to discourage abusive messages, and participants are invited to complain to moderators about any messages they feel are inappropriate. Online reactions to participants who contribute apparently irrelevant remarks or who are uncooperative in other ways may be quite severe. Common reasons for being reproached (or *flamed*) include *shouting* (sending messages in upper case).

Message boards are net forums to which people can post messages at a more leisurely pace, often over days or weeks. The fact that the communication is in this case *asynchronous* can be seen from the extract below, where the date and time when each participant posted their message is recorded:

Who else gets our TV and Radio? The Debater – 233rd post – 2 Feb 2004 20:22
Just watched the 'Space' programme on BBC 2. I was fascinated when they mentioned TV and Radio signals reach out into space. How far do these signals go? Has anybody picked up our endless chatter do you think? [reply]

re: Who else gets our TV and Radio? Skywalker – 70th post – 3 Feb 2004 12:40
Well, if you say that we have been broadcasting radio signals for about a hundred years and TV for about sixty, that means that radio signals have travelled one hundred light years out into space and TV signals sixty light years. Both well into our immediate cosmic neighbourhood. The bad news: they could never be heard or viewed by any alien civilisations as the signals would not be coherent over such distances due to their weakness. Extraterrestrials sufficiently advanced would be able to identify the signals as artificial, but there's no prospect of them reconstructing the signals so they can sit down to watch 'I'm A Celebrity, Get Me Out Of Here' at some point in the future. Which is probably a good thing, as it would instantly disprove the idea of there being intelligent life on Earth. [reply]

re: Who else gets our TV and Radio? The Imbiber – 34th post – 3 Feb 2004 14:22
I presume you have seen the film 'Contact', based on Carl Sagan's book. Aliens had picked up the first radio signal from Earth of any strength, which happened to be of the opeining of the 1938 Berlin Olympics. [reply]

re: Who else gets our TV and Radio? Skywalker – 79th post – 3 Feb 2004 15:39
I haven't seen the film but I did read the book many years ago when it came out. Interesting. [reply]

re: Who else gets our TV and Radio? Marshall – 262nd post – 3 Feb 2004 19:38
'. . . which happened to be of the opeining of the 1938 Berlin Olympics.'
Yes, and the aliens beamed the TV signal back but with a load of extra technical information stuffed in between the video frames. Maybe that's what the BBC has done with the Horizon programmes? If not, it seems like an awful waste of space. ;-)

re: Who else gets our TV and Radio? Starstruck – 64th post – 3 Feb 2004 20:27
The Berlin Olympics were in 1936 NOT 1938. [reply]

re: Who else gets our TV and Radio? Rover – 314th post – 4 Feb 2004 21:50
If an alien was to receive any of our tv or radio signals would it be apparent that they were artificial? With tv in particular do you think they would be able to decode the signal and recreate the image? [reply]

(Participants' online identities have been changed)
(Adapted from the BBC 'Science Message Board')

The 'thread' or discussion represented in this extract extended over two days, with most of the messages posted on one day but at intervals of an hour or longer. What is interesting about the discussion is that although some of the characteristic features of electronic English are present (the emoticon ;-) ; lower case for *tv*, upper case for *NOT 1938*; typing error in **opeining*), most of the messages appear to have been composed quite carefully, some with a degree of attention to grammar, spelling and punctuation that would have been appropriate in letter-writing. Of course, the messages still have a conversational tone, reflected in the following aspects:

- the use of *Well* and *Yes*.
- the use of ellipsis, as in *Just watched the 'Space' programme on BBC2* (omitting the subject 'I' and auxiliary 'have'), *The bad news* (omitting 'This is' or 'Here is') and *Interesting* (omitting 'it was').

- the tendency to use punctuation to reflect the rhythm of speech rather than to ensure that every sentence is grammatically complete, for example in *Which is probably a good thing, as it would instantly disprove the idea of there being intelligent life on Earth* (here a relative pronoun begins a new sentence, rather than the demonstrative pronoun *This* or a noun phrase such as *This fact*).
- The placement of *do you think* at the end of a question to create an impression of a 'spoken' exchange, as in *Has anybody picked up our endless chatter do you think?* (instead of *Do you think anybody has picked up our endless chatter?*)

7.8 Summary

In this chapter we have seen that speech, writing and the new media are interrelated in often complex ways. Speech may be like writing in some situations, and writing like speech in others. Email, text messages and online discussions have features in common with both spoken and written language yet they are essentially much more than hybrid media. Electronic English has its own varieties and sub-varieties, breaking new ground in communicative styles and reflecting the energy and creativity of its communities of users worldwide.

Activities

1. Ask two people to think of a joke or short anecdote. Record one of them telling their joke to you, and ask the other to write theirs down. Compare the recording and the written text. What stylistic features can you identify in each that reflect the medium of communication? Now use the recording you have made to practise transcribing speech, using the conventions for orthographic (non-phonetic) transcription explained in this chapter.
2. Here is a simulated conversation of the kind often to be found in coursebooks for English as a Foreign Language. As you read it, consider how far it succeeds in imitating typical conversational features:

Bob	Well, well, well. I don't believe it. It's Karen, isn't it? Karen Mills?
Karen	Bob Atkinson. How nice to see you. I haven't seen you since – oh, when was it ? – Jane and Dave's wedding.
Bob	Yes, that's right. That must be nearly twelve years now. Good heavens! Doesn't time fly?
Karen	You've put on weight!

Bob	Yes, well, you know how it is. Too much easy living. Anyway, what are you up to these days? Are you still working for that bank?
Karen	Bank?
Bob	Didn't you use to work for a bank?
Karen	Oh, yes, the bank. Well, it was a building society actually. No, I left there ages ago. I thought it was time to see the world!
Bob	And did you? See the world, I mean.
Karen	Well, parts of it. I went to Japan first and then China for a year.
Bob	Sounds great. What were you doing there?
Karen	I was teaching English. But then I came back to Britain and I worked in a theatre for a while and then did a few other jobs.
Bob	So what are you doing now?

3. Collect some samples of English from online chat and/or message boards. What rules of communication do the contributors appear to follow? Can you tell what age group they belong to or whether they have specific interests in common? If so, do these factors seem to you to affect the way they communicate? How polite or otherwise are they towards one another and/or newcomers? Are abbreviations and acronyms used, and if so, can you understand them?

Further Reading

Cornbleet and Carter (2001) is an accessible introduction to the formal and functional differences between speech and writing. Short (1996) provides an interesting and practical discussion of the relationship between conversation and drama. Ideas for project work on conversation analysis can be found in Wray, Trott and Bloomer (1998). For an extended study of the history of written English up to and including email, see Baron (2000). For an exploration of computer-mediated language see Crystal (2001).

Chapter 8

English in Context

8.1 Introduction

In my own studies of varieties of English I have always particularly enjoyed exploring how the language can vary according to the context or situation in which it is used. This is a rich area for investigation and one that illustrates just how versatile and creative language is, how many purposes it can serve and also how it is affected by non-linguistic factors such as the relationship between the people communicating and the aim or function of the communication.

A starting point for the study of context in language variation is to consider, in your own use of language, how you adjust the way you speak or write according to all kinds of external factors. Just think of a typical day and of all the possible situations in which you use language: you might, for instance, talk to fellow students or your family over breakfast; take part in a seminar; write notes for yourself in a lecture; converse informally with your friends in a coffee bar; participate in a sport; go shopping and so on. Obviously, you don't use your language in the same way in all these situations but make all kinds of spontaneous adjustments to your pronunciation, vocabulary, grammar and level of formality, so that your speech or writing is appropriate to the context, or at least as appropriate as you want it to be. In some situations you will be more conscious of the need to use your language appropriately than in others. For instance, in the case of taking notes for yourself, you might produce what would be an indecipherable scrawl to anyone else, yet to you it will make sense, so this doesn't matter. However, an indecipherable scawl *would* matter if you were writing a note to your tutor to explain your absence from class or the late submission of an essay, since it would indicate a lack of care in writing the note and probably suggest to your tutor that the explanation might not be genuine.

All this is quite straightforward, but the trouble with the word *context* is that it has a number of meanings in everyday usage, not all of which are helpful to us in studying language varieties. One meaning of context in everyday speech is the circumstances and conditions relevant to a particular action, event or fact. Although not far from what we mean by context in linguistics, this sense can be misleading, since synonyms such as 'circumstances' or 'conditions' fail to tell us precisely enough what exactly we need to describe when we look at contextual variation and why we need to describe it. For example, in an exchange between a doctor and patient, would a view of context as simply 'circumstances' include just the physical setting (hospital ward? doctor's surgery?) or also the purpose of the exchange (to discuss symptoms? alternative treatments?). Would it also include, for instance, the topic being spoken about (pregnancy? suspected cancer?) and whether or not the exchange was face to face? Another everyday use of context occurs, for example, when politicians and other public figures accuse reporters of quoting their remarks 'out of context', or not making it clear what words preceded or followed the quoted part. Context is not usually used in this sense in linguistics; instead the term *co-text* is sometimes applied to the verbal or linguistic context (as opposed to the situational context) of a particular sound, word, phrase, clause, sentence, paragraph, or even a longer stretch of text.

The purpose of this chapter will be to outline more systematic ways of interpreting context for language study, as well as to discuss other, sometimes equally problematical, terms that we need to use in exploring contextual variation.

8.2 Speech situations

Before going any further we should briefly recall our discussion in Chapter 1 about variation relating to speech communities or social networks. There we saw that our language varies according to the groups we belong to and interact with, and that most of us are members of a number of social networks, for example, our immediate community, colleagues, friends and those with whom we share particular interests or hobbies.

Clearly, most of the situations in which we interact, whether in speech, writing or other media, are connected with these social networks. In other words, a conversation between members of a youth gang is likely to differ markedly from a conversation between, say, travellers on a train. The members of the gang will normally use a shared 'code' of some kind – slang expressions that signal their shared affiliation and that may not be understood by outsiders. No such 'code' would be shared by a random group of travellers temporarily sharing the compartment of a train. Therefore, these two communicative situations are clearly quite distinct from a contextual point of view. And to look properly at contextual variation, we need to be able to break each of them down in ways that will effectively reveal the differences between them.

One well-known model of the situational factors that influence conversational interaction was devised by Dell Hymes (1972). Hymes was an anthropological linguist and his main interest was in investigating the influence of 'rules of speaking' within different cultures and describing from an ethnographic perspective the language of formal, set events such as weddings and welcoming ceremonies. However, Hymes's categories (which use the mnemonic S P E A K I N G) can still be useful in drawing our attention to the fundamentals of interaction. Also, although originally intended for the analysis of instances of *spoken* communication (which Hymes himself called 'speech events'), the categories can be applied quite successfully to most 'communicative' situations. Here is the basic model:

Components of a speech situation

S   **setting** and scene of a speech situation, distinguishing between the physical locale and type of activity

P   **participants**, often characterised by terms such as addresser, addressee, speaker, performer, audience, questioner, answerer, caller, interviewee, etc.

E   **ends**, including both functions and outcomes; functions may be broadly classified as *transactional* (if the content of talk is important) or *interactional* (if talk serves to reinforce or establish social or personal relations); outcomes have to do with what effect the speech has on the addressee or other aspect of the situation

A   **act** sequence, including the content and form of speech

K   **key**, tone, mood or manner (e.g. serious, formal, sarcastic, and so on)

I   **instrumentalities**, including the 'channel' or medium (e.g. speech, writing, face to face, email) and 'code' (language and/or variety used)

N   **norms** of interaction and interpretation (the basic rules that seem to underlie the interaction)

G   **genre**, any of a class of named speech acts (greeting, leave-taking, sermon, lecture, joke, and so on)

(Adapted from O'Grady, Dobrovolsky and Katamba (1997))

The best way to put the framework to the test is to think of any communicative situation and try to describe it according to Hymes's categories. Here, for example, is how the model might be applied to an interview for an academic post:

> Setting: the physical setting would normally be a room arranged to allow the interview panel to see and address the interviewee, possibly seated around a table. As a type of activity, the interview is an important and strictly controlled event.

> Participants: these would be the candidate plus interviewers, usually chaired by a person of higher institutional rank, such as a Dean or Head of Faculty. Essentially, the interviewers would have the role of questioners, the candidate that of an answerer.

> Ends: here we would highlight the *transactional* function (since what the candidate actually said would be of central importance), though parts of the interview

would also have an interactional function (to establish a friendly atmosphere and to put the candidate at ease). The outcomes would include the effect of the questions on the candidate and of the candidate's responses on the panel.

Act Sequence: we would expect a formal sequence of introductions by the Chair, followed by a controlled question-and-answer sequence in which the candidate would normally have the longest speaking turns, followed by a formal closing by the Chair of the panel.

Key: a professional, serious tone would be expected, though attempts might be made to reduce tension (e.g. through some use of informal language and/or some of the reassuring features of ordinary conversation). Members of the panel would probably try to avoid appearing to read from a prepared set of questions.

Instrumentalities: we would expect a spoken standard variety of the language to be used, along with academic and subject-specific discourse (e.g. vocabulary drawn from the field of physics or literary criticism). In certain circumstances, a candidate might be given an interview with the help of video-conferencing facilities – this would be described here as a specific 'channel' of communication.

Norms: there would be norms of polite address in operation (use of titles like *Doctor* and *Professor*). In a formal interview, turn-taking is controlled by the Chair, who may signal verbally or by eye contact, nodding, etc. when it is a particular interviewer's turn to ask the interviewee questions. The interviewee can also signal when they are ready for the questioning to be handed over to someone else. Topic-shifting would be mostly under the control of the panel, but the development of the topics would be the responsibility of the candidate.

Genre: an academic interview is a sub-genre of the professional interview. It will therefore have some things in common with, say, an interview for a managerial post in a service industry, as well as with other kinds of interview in the education sector (e.g. schoolteaching post).

The S P E A K I N G model might appear to cover just about all the possible factors influencing our spoken behaviour in a particular context. However, its usefulness is primarily in providing a *descriptive* framework, not an *interpretative* one, and we need to remember that while speakers are always influenced by the situation in which they find themselves, they also have aims and intentions behind what they say and how they say it. Hymes's model was intended for the study of rather ritualised speech situations in which speakers could be expected to follow the rules of interaction laid down by their speech communities. In a wedding ceremony, for example, individual participants follow set ways of speaking, as established in their culture and community, so we can analyse such situations fairly easily with Hymes's model (they have a very clear 'act sequence' and equally describable 'ends' and 'norms', for instance). Ordinary conversation, by contrast, is far less rigid than this and allows speakers more freedom to influence the interaction in certain ways, depending on their individual feelings and intentions. Speakers interact in ways that cannot simply be put down to 'norms', and their actual words and intended meanings may not match up in the way that happens (or is supposed to happen anyway) in official or ceremonial contexts. The study of what speakers may mean and how they are understood (i.e. the study of pragmatics) goes beyond our present concern with situational context. However, the way we describe situational context clearly needs to take account of the fact that speakers do not simply 'respond' passively to the situations in which they find themselves, but can actively 'shape' those situations through their use of language.

8.3   Register

Register is a useful concept in the study of language in context. Spolsky (1998:34) writes:

> A register is a variety of language most likely to be used in a specific situation and with particular roles and statuses involved. Examples might be a toast at a wedding, sports broadcast, or talking to a baby. A register is marked by choices of vocabulary and of other aspects of style.

The term 'register' is connected to language variation according to use, rather than to variation according to the user, for which we have the term 'dialect'. However, while we might choose, as in this chapter, to focus more on one type of variation than the other at any particular time, the two are not mutually exclusive. Indeed, as Leech, Deuchar and Hoogenraad (1982:10) note, 'dialect and register variation interact with each other since both the dimensions of user and use are always present'.

A theory of register associated principally with Halliday (e.g. 1973) identified three dimensions of a communicative event: the *field, tenor* and *mode* of discourse. The *field* is the social activity, purpose and sometimes subject-matter in the communicative situation. In a live tennis match commentary the field is identifiable on the linguistic and stylistic level by its vocabulary (in this context we expect to find lexical items like *lob, deuce* and *match point*) and specific grammatical features such as a large number of clauses with action predicates. This is especially true of radio sports commentary, where the ongoing state of play is supplemented by more detailed comments on the precise actions and styles of the players, as in *Capriati serves another brilliant ace*. Action predicates are typically linked with the surrounding nouns, with the agent role normally taken by the initial noun phrase in the clause, as in the Capriati example above.

Tenor refers to the social roles of the participants and their interrelationships. The linguistic and stylistic features associated with tenor are mainly *mood, deixis* and *modality*. *Mood*, in Hallidayan, or systemic, grammar refers to distinctions of *illocutionary force* or communicative function in sentence types, shown partly by whether sentences use an indicative (stating), imperative (commanding/requesting) or interrogative (questioning) mood. *Deixis*, from the Greek for 'pointing' or 'showing', refers to the orientational features of language connected with space, time and viewpoint. Deictic words have variable or shifting meanings depending on the identity of the speaker. The precise meanings of *this, that, these, those, here, there, yesterday, now, I, you, the former, the latter, etc.* can only be worked out through awareness of their context of utterance. Finally, *modality* is that aspect of linguistic structure which deals with the speaker's degree of knowledge or certainty about propositions, communicated through modal verbs such as *must, may, can, will* and also through adverbs like *presumably, possibly* or through other expressions of certainty, obligation, etc. such as *I'm quite sure* we're on the right road or *Passengers are not permitted to smoke during take-off or landing.*

The third dimension of register, **mode**, refers to the medium (spoken or written), and sometimes also channel, of communication (e.g. mobile phone). This dimension is associated with the textual function of language, with textual cohesion, textual development, types of emphasis, etc. and also the part that genre, if identifiable, might play in the text's overall organisation. On the level of linguistic and stylistic features, we are concerned here with a number of possible items. For example, various cohesive ties (e.g. pronoun reference, substitution, connecting adverbials like *however* or *as a result*) link sentences into larger units, helping to create overall coherence in a text. Thematisation, or what elements are placed initially in the clause, helps to indicate the emphasis or prominent aspects of a message: for example, in *Above the fireplace stood a very large oil painting* (where the 'theme' or initial element is the adverbial *Above the fireplace*), the end focus and most important part of the message is *a very large oil painting*. Finally, typographic style and possible genre-markers such as rhyme in verse or headlines in newspapers are also linked with mode.

Within the broader social context of communication we need to bear in mind that many discourses today are multi-modal and combine linguistic with non-linguistic sign systems such as photography, film, computer graphics and music. This use of a range of semiotic systems is shown very clearly in TV commercials, where it would be inadequate to focus only on what is spoken or on text to be read on the screen. While context and language are the main focus of this chapter, it is therefore worth emphasising that non-linguistic practices also make meanings and that these need to be set alongside those of linguistic interaction if we are to have a more comprehensive picture of how certain texts communicate and how their meanings may be understood or inferred.

The distinctions among field, tenor and mode provide us with a way of breaking down a communicative situation to help us answer, respectively, the *what, who* and *how* of the language produced in it. Essentially, these dimensions of register ask us to find out *what* is actually happening in terms of subject matter or activity; *who* the participants are and how they relate to one another; and *how* they are using language, consciously or unconsciously, to respond to and shape the situation they are in.

113

8.3.1 Register analysis

To illustrate different registers we will now look at a few texts from some well-known social domains and consider them from the point of view of field, tenor and mode:

PEPPERED COD STEAKS

Serves 4   240 kcals per portion

White bread – *4 slices*
Ground mixed peppercorns – *1 tbsp*
Paprika – *½ tsp*
Flaked almonds – *50g (2oz)*
Cod fillet steaks – *4*
Egg – *1, beaten*

METHOD
1. Pre-heat oven to 200° C/400° F/Gas 6.
2. Place the bread into a food processor and whizz to achieve a fine crumb.
3. In a large bowl, combine the breadcrumbs, peppercorns, paprika and almonds.
4. Dip the cod fillets into the egg and coat with the crumb mix. Place fillets onto a greased baking sheet and bake in the oven for 15–20 minutes or until golden.

• *Serve with Hollandaise sauce and salad*

While the social domain from which this text comes can be described broadly as 'cookery', its field of discourse is, more specifically, that of instruction. Instruction texts, whether about using a computer, assembling a bookcase from a flatpack or applying for a new passport, all have a practical aim and their language needs to be clear and direct. There is field-specific vocabulary (e.g. *food processor, fillets, Hollandaise sauce*) as well as words used with specific meanings, such as *fine, coat* and *beaten*. Other field-related features are the use of abbreviations (e.g. *kcals* for . . . 'Calories'; *tbsp* for 'tablespoon'; *tsp* for 'teaspoon'). Grammatically, the 'ingredients' section of the recipe is a list of noun phrases (*Ground mixed peppercorns; Flaked almonds*), with some nouns coming before their modifiers as in *Egg – 1, beaten* (rather than *1 beaten egg*) . In the 'Method' section the predominant clause pattern follows the sequence Predicator or verbal element (P) Object (O) Adverbial (A), with clauses normally joined by the coordinating conjunction *and*. This allows the second clause in the sequence to omit the Object, shown by the symbol ø below, as this is recoverable from the first clause as follows:

P   O   A   (conj) P   A
(Dip) (the cod fillets) (into the egg) (and) (coat) ø (with the crumb mix)

P	O	A	(conj)	P	A
(Place)	*(fillets)*	*(onto a greased baking sheet)*	*(and)*	*(bake)*	ø *(in the oven)*

The symbol ø represents the 'understood' *the cod fillets* in the first sentence and *fillets* in the second.

With regard to the tenor of the register the imperative mood is predominant (*Pre-heat . . . ; Dip . . . ; place . . . ; serve . . .*). Words normally considered to be deictic or orientational in function (e.g. *here* or *this*) do not occur, and features of modality such as modal verbs or adverbs are not present in this recipe. Finally, regarding the mode of the register, the recipe is cohesive and coherent largely through its genre-specific layout (the original also has a photo of the cooked cod steaks to the right of the recipe), its numbering of steps in the method, and the use of the definite article to refer back to nouns mentioned earlier (e.g. in step 2 of the Method *the bread* refers back to *White bread* in the list of ingredients). In addition, there is much use of lexical links such as the connection between *fine crumb*, *breadcrumbs* and *crumb mix*. In terms of thematisation, the text typically has the verb (predicator) as the initial element in the clause, though there is one instance of an adverbial as theme: *In a large bowl, combine the breadcrumbs. . . .*

The next text we shall look at is taken from a leaflet provided by a high street bank to customers:

17. General Provisions

17.1 The Bank reserves the right at all times to supplement, amend, or vary these Conditions of Use as a result of a requirement of law, customer feedback, or product development or such other reason as is communicated to You at the time of notification of change. Any such change will be effective upon notice to You and notice shall be given by any means the Bank sees fit as permitted by law. On receipt of such notification, You may terminate this Agreement in accordance with Condition 16.1.

We might assume that the field of this text is, simply, banking. However, this would be too broad a description, since banking can also cover many other types of discourse, for example face-to-face exchanges across the counter between clerks and customers, or meetings between managers and other staff. Here, the field is the legal terms and conditions of the service the bank is providing. This field is marked by a tendency towards nominalised structures such as *On receipt of such notification* (rather than the more conversational *When you receive such notification*), as well as legal terminology such as *reserves the right*, *will be effective upon notice to You*, and *terminate this Agreement*. There is frequent use of abstract nouns (*requirement*, *change*, *law*) and some formulaic expressions such as *at all times*. This text is not, however, a document relating solely to law, but also to the bank itself as a company, as is shown by the phrases *customer feedback* and *product development*, which belong to the field of business management.

The tenor of the register is very formal. It uses the indicative mood consistently as it is concerned with factual statements and would not, for example, wish to solicit the opinion of the reader by asking a question. The text's modality is signalled both lexically (*a requirement of law* = the law says it <u>must</u> be done; *as permitted by law* = the law says it <u>can</u> be done; *in accordance with Condition 16.1* = in accordance with what Condition 16.1 says <u>must</u> be done) and through the use of the auxiliaries *will*, *shall* and *may* (meaning 'are permitted to').

The mode of the text is clearly written, with the layout and small typeface typical of documents outlining detailed terms and conditions. Although reference is facilitated through numbered paragraphs with subsections, the text is not intended to be attractively presented or to encourage reading out of general interest (in total contrast to the layout of an advertisement, for instance). There is also a distinctive use of capitalisation for the most important words, such as *Bank, Conditions of Use, You, Agreement*. Since the terms and conditions described are legally enforceable, the language must avoid ambiguity at all costs. This means that cohesion is created through the repetition of key lexical items (*Any such change will be effective upon <u>notice</u> to You and <u>notice</u> shall be given by any means* . . .) rather than through pronoun referencing or use of synonyms, both of which might result in a lack of clarity. However, marked themes may also assist cohesion, as in <u>*On receipt of such notification,*</u> *You may* . . . , where the adverbial element is placed first in the clause so that an immediate link is made to *notice shall be given* in the previous sentence.

The fact that the terms and conditions are addressed to the lay reader rather than legal experts ensures that this text is not, by any means, the most inaccessible example of legal language. It avoids archaisms, for instance, and excessively long and complicated sentences. It also retains punctuation to aid reading, unlike certain legal texts, such as statutes or wills, which use punctuation more sparingly, often omitting commas in lists or reserving the use of full stops to the end of key sections or even a complete document. However, the text still retains many of the characteristic features of the language of the law, a field in which traditional and conservative usage plays an important part.

8.3.2 Register combinations

Some types of discourse, such as advertising, literary or institutional (e.g. company) texts, can be multi-vocal in that they systematically borrow, switch and mix registers for a range of purposes. Advertisements, for example, while needing to remain recognisable (ultimately) as advertisements, frequently borrow and exploit other registers. For example, in the following advertisement for Olivio (a blended spread with butter and olive oil) I have underlined the parts that are taken from another register, which you will probably recognise as the language of the Christian marriage ceremony: '<u>*TO HAVE AND TO HOLD*</u> *ON WARM CRUMPETS* <u>*FROM THIS DAY*</u> <u>*FORTH*</u>'. <u>*We are gathered here today to witness the joining together of*</u> *creamy butter* *and Mediterranean olive oil. Truly a marriage made in heaven. <u>CELEBRATE THIS UNION</u>.* This is an unusual and entertaining use of a register with fixed and sometimes archaic (*from this day forth*) forms of language for the purpose of selling a product totally unrelated to weddings. The use of the ceremonial register when talking about this everyday product evokes positive images in the mind of the reader, who is encouraged to transfer associations of love, devotion and lifetime allegiance to the Olivio spread! Another way in which many advertisements can create positive associations through register-mixing is by borrowing stylistically from narrative genres. The following example is an advertisement for Glenmorangie Scotch whisky:

> It was Christmas Eve and the annual Glenmorangie party was in full swing. Somewhere a door opened. A sudden waft of icy Firthside air provoked a flurry of goosepimples. And a briskly pedalling figure disappeared into the mist out-side. 'Who was that?' asked a visitor. 'Oh, only George Mackenzie. He's away up to the mash-house to tend the mash.'
>
> Even those who do not work at the distillery know of George's dedication to the mash. Ask him why on Christmas Eve, Burns' Night, even Hogmanay he will give up all to be with his charge, and he will reply: 'Time and the mash wait for no man.'

This text uses a quaint, old-fashioned storytelling style strategically to highlight a Scottish setting and weather (*Firthside, icy, goosepimples, mist*), Scottish dialect (illustrated by the construction *'He's away up to . . .'*), stereotyped culture (the poet Robert Burns; the Scottish New Year or 'Hogmanay' celebrations), the secrecy of the fermenting process (*mash*), as well as the special attention lavished on the product (*give up all to be with his charge*). Mackenzie's reply finally encloses the image of the whisky within the reassuring 'warmth' of apparently proverbial wisdom (adapting the actual proverb *time and tide wait for no man*).

The freedom to draw on other registers is particularly obvious in literary texts. Though a novel may be expected to tell us some kind of story, it does so through a multitude of different 'voices' and is essentially *heteroglossic*, a translation of the Russian term *raznorecie* coined by Mikhail Bakhtin) or composed of many interacting dialects and registers (see Bakhtin 1981).

Here is an extract from a novel in which the presence of, and interaction between, different registers is quite striking:

> A coroner's court is a court of law; though an inquest is not a trial. But my father, a simple and impressionable man, summoned by the coroner's office to attend as witness, was under every apprehension that he stood accused; that the purpose of this official gathering was not to ascertain how Freddie Parr had died but how he, Henry Crick, lock-keeper of the Atkinson Lock, had by his own negligence suffered a sixteen-year-old boy to drown in his sluice and had further compounded his crime by defacing the body of the same with a boat-hook. My father, in a hot courtroom, in an unaccustomed stiff collar under which the sweat prickled and tickled, awaited the judgement: Henry Crick, we

find you guilty of manslaughter, of murder, of death, of the sins and wrongs of all the world . . .

> . . . CORONER: At what time, in your opinion, did death occur?
> PATHOLOGIST: As near as I can judge, between the hours of 11p.m. of the twenty-fifth and 1 a.m. of the twenty-sixth.
> CORONER: Mr Crick, between those hours, did you hear any sounds to alarm you – splashings, cries for help – in the vicinity of the lock?
> MY FATHER: No sir. I'm afraid, sir, I was asleep . . .
> CORONER: Doctor, the wound and contusion on the right side of the deceased's face – can you explain how and when they were caused?
> PATHOLOGIST: By a rigid, semi-sharp object or instrument, some hours after death had occurred.
> CORONER: On the last point you are sure?
> PATHOLOGIST: Yes, sir.
> CORONER: Mr Crick, could you give your account of how exactly this wound came to be caused?
> MY FATHER: He were heavy. I'm sorry, sir. The boat-hook slipped – got him.
> CORONER (patiently): Do not be sorry, Mr Crick – but be more precise. Rest assured, you have no cause to reproach yourself in this matter . . .

But my father does not rest assured. He walks up and down the tow-path asking WHYwhywhy. He asks, how do these things happen? . . . He casts back over his life (just as I, one day, will cast back over his life, going even so far as to unearth dusty inquest transcripts), looking for wrongs requiring expiation, omens to be fulfilled.

(Graham Swift, 1983 *Waterland* revised edition 1992,
London and Basingstoke: Pan Books Ltd, in association
with William Heinemann Ltd)

The first thing we notice about this extract is the switch halfway through from third-person narrative to an apparent 'transcript' of courtroom proceedings. Within the extract as a whole, the most dominant register is that of the courtroom (*had by his own negligence, between the hours of 11 p.m. of the twenty-fifth and 1 a.m. of the twenty-sixth*, etc.), contrasting starkly with Henry Crick's non-standard dialect (*He were heavy*) and the narrator's sympathetic description of his too easily cowed and vulnerable father (*in an unaccustomed stiff collar under which the sweat prickled and tickled; He walks up and down the tow-path asking WHYwhywhy*). The narrator shows by introducing the courtroom register that the language of the inquest is in itself enough to frighten his father. However, by also quoting the coroner's phrase *Rest assured* in *But my father does not rest assured*, he suggests that Mr Crick is vulnerable not only to the register of the court but also to that of the educated classes, who immediately daunt a man like Crick, even when they are trying to avoid excessive formality and to reassure him. As this extract shows, *Waterland* is a work that shows fascination with the existence and interplay of different registers and with how our experience of the world is mediated through varieties of language.

The satire and parody to be found in much popular journalism are among the most interesting varieties in which registers tend to be combined. The following is an example of a text that mixes registers for this purpose. As you read it, consider what specific features of vocabulary and grammar, etc. can be identified as typical of the borrowed register, and what makes them effective in their 'new' context?

Modern recipes: No 21
Costume drama
1 classic text
1 large tub whimsy
3lb mixed anachronisms
1 gross britches
2 gross frocks
7 tins potted ham
1 garden
1 Helena Bonham Carter
(or own-brand equivalent)

TAKE the classic text and age by the time-honoured process of using it to bore generations of schoolchildren. When thoroughly steeped in apathy, adapt it with a filleting knife and a lump hammer, taking care to discard all nuance, literary elegance and distinctive dialogue.

When only Mills & Boon plot is left, lard thoroughly with whimsy until gullet rises. Pepper with anachronisms, which should include at least 30 per cent psychobabble. Carefully landscape the garden and fill with pathways. Fill the britches and frocks with ham and perambulate through the garden, turning every few minutes and basting with intrigue (ask your retailer for extra-insipid strength). For a slightly novel flavour, place the garden in South America, but don't stint on the britches and frocks.

Bake at gas mark $\frac{1}{2}$ until tepid. Garnish with Helena Bonham Carter. Serve to eager audience of former bored schoolchildren. Export leftovers to America.

As a complement to the meal, reissue classic text in shiny new cover featuring garden, pathways, britches, frocks, ham and Helena Bonham Carter. Decorate with sticker reading: 'As seen on BBC1/ITV/Sky Movies/The Nude Windsurfing Channel' (delete as appropriate).

(David Bennum, copyright Guardian Newspapers Limited 1997)

The essential purpose of this text is to mock well-known film adaptations of classic literary works such as the novels of E. M. Forster. In particular, it targets the films made by Ismael Merchant and James Ivory, or Merchant Ivory Productions (e.g. *Howards End*, 1993, starring Anthony Hopkins, Vanessa Redgrave, Helena Bonham Carter and Emma Thompson). Helena Bonham Carter starred in a romantic role in several of the films – hence the reference to her in this text. In order to accentuate the fact that such films appear to share certain predictable 'ingredients' which are mixed in a rather formulaic way, the text exploits the typical discourse of 'the recipe' (see the first example in 8.3.1 above), giving apparent instructions which anyone wishing to produce a film of this kind should follow. The simple layout of a recipe, with ingredients followed by the 'Method', is of course ideally suited to conveying the underlying message that anyone, regardless of talent, could produce a box office hit according to the costume drama pattern. And an important aspect of the joke is that Ismael Merchant is not only a film director but also well known as a cook. He has published cookery books and merchandises a brand of food.

The borrowed register provides scope for a great deal of punning word-play, e.g. *gross*, meaning both inclusive number and, as an adjective, un-attractively large and repulsive; *ham*, meaning both meat and excessively theatrical acting, as in to 'ham it up' or 'ham actor', as well as thighs and buttocks, as in *Fill the britches with ham*. Both *filleting knife* and *lump hammer* encourage the notion that costume drama treats the classic text with 'violent' insensitivity. Other cookery terms also support the satirical purpose, e.g. *steeped, lard . . . with, pepper, turning, basting, flavour, Bake, tepid, Garnish, Serve, leftovers,* reinforcing the idea that the success of costume drama lies in what you throw into the mixture before handing it, as it were, on a plate to an eager and undiscriminating consumer. The allusion to *own-brand equivalent* suggests that even the heroine may be more cheaply duplicated, if preferred. Of course, a full analysis of this text would do more than break down its use of register-mixing. We could also see its purpose as being to entertain a readership assumed to be culturally elitist and critical of cinema box office successes. The allusions to *Helena Bonham Carter, Mills & Boon* (a company that publishes best-selling popular romances) and *Export leftovers to America* make it clear that the implied reader is British or very familiar with British cultural life and humour.

8.4 Summary

In this chapter our focus has been on the fundamentals of English in context and on some of the key terminology used to describe speech situations and general areas of language use. We have considered the influence of context in relatively straightforward situations such as the giving of instructions, as well as more sophisticated contexts in which language may masquerade as belonging to a specific social domain when it is in fact only borrowing that domain's linguistic clothes for purposes of its own. Throughout this chapter I have been wary of drawing oversimplified conclusions about the influence of external context on language, since speakers usually have some freedom to influence and shape the context in which they find themselves. The questions of how variation in English can be connected not just to the known context but also to speakers' attitudes and choices within it, and more broadly to issues of power in language, will be the subject of the next chapter.

Activities

1. Apply the S P E A K I N G mnemonic to three different situations in which you have used your language over the past week (e.g. one formal, one informal, one less straightforward). You could, for instance, select an enquiry you might have made at an office of some kind, a phone call to a friend, or a conversation with a small child.

2. Analyse the following description of an owl by considering the features of its register according to the dimensions of field, tenor and mode:

   BARN OWL *Tyto alba*

   Du – Kerkuil
   Ge – Schleiereule
   Fr – Chouette effraie
   Sw – Tornuggla   **Plate 64**

   Identification: 14″ (35cm.). Medium-sized, very pale owl, with a distinctive heart-shaped face, tapering lower body and long visible legs. Hunting flight usually low, slow, buoyant but characteristically wavering, as bird looks down intently for small rodents. Upper-parts golden-buff, sullied grey and finely speckled; face white, with dark eyes; under-parts mainly white in W. and S. Perches upright, with 'knock-kneed' stance. Nocturnal but often hunts by day in winter.
   Voice: Long, wild shriek. Hissing, snoring and yapping notes also given,
   Habitat: Very partial to human habitation, breeding in farm buildings, church towers, ruins, etc. Also frequents parks with old timber, occasionally cliffs.
   Map 191.

   (From *Collins Field Guide: Birds of Britain and Europe* (5th ed. 1993)
   by Roger Tory Peterson, Guy Mountfort and P.A.D. Hollom,
   London: HarperCollins)

3. Find two or three texts (e.g. advertisements) which combine registers in various ways, and discuss the linguistic and stylistic effects produced by this combination. Consider the aims of the texts and how the use of more than one register contributes to these aims.

Further Reading

Thorne (1997) provides illustrative analyses of a number of use-related varieties of English, including the language of newspapers, advertising, law and politics. Holmes (2001) includes a section on use-related language variation, looking in particular at stylistic choices reflecting the attitudes of speakers to each other. Fowler (1996) is well worth consulting on different kinds of register combination in literary texts, as is Short (1996) on style variation in literature. See also Biber and Finegan (1994).

Chapter 9

English and Power

I'd like to begin this chapter with two key questions:

> *What do we mean by 'power' in language?*
> *Are there powerful varieties?*

These two questions are closely related. Unless we are clear about the various ways in which speakers (or writers) can achieve or lose power through their use of English, we cannot decide whether we should call certain varieties of the language intrinsically more or less powerful than others. In considering the first question, we might initially propose that power in language means saying things in forceful ways, for example saying *I demand an immediate reply* rather than *I hope to hear from you soon*. Obviously, we can, if we wish, use words and expressions that instantly signal forcefulness, resistance, insistence and all sorts of other 'strong' attitudes. However, it would be simplistic to assume that we are powerful speakers *only* when we use language of this kind. Indeed, we all know that it is often more likely that we will get what we want if we use polite or more cooperative language, and that using overtly forceful language could get us into a lot of trouble. So, on a very basic level, we can say immediately that power in language is not the same as aggressive talk.

A second assumption we might make in defining power in language is that it is essentially the speech or writing of 'powerful' people. By 'powerful people' we might, for instance, mean government ministers or those who head large organisations and are assumed to have an important say in the way the economy is run. Or we might include people in positions of authority, such as prison officers, the police, inspectors or teachers, and assume, for instance, that a prison officer is automatically a more powerful speaker than a prisoner. In fact, although there is a degree of ordinary logic in this assumption, it is linguistically flawed, since no speaker can be assumed to be automatically or continuously powerful in all interactional contexts. Let us look at the example of the prison officer and the prisoner more carefully. In certain circumstances, the power that the guard officially has over the prisoner (e.g. the power to give a negative report on the prisoner's behaviour) could be challenged by the prisoner. For instance, the prisoner might be in a position to make a formal complaint against the prison officer, unless the latter makes some concessions, permitting the prisoner to have more freedom in certain ways, or turning a blind eye to certain types of rule-breaking within the prison regime. This situation could result in an interaction between the two in which power was no longer just on the one side, but being 'negotiated' by both parties. Indeed, the successful running of a modern prison depends not on a relentlessly forceful imposition of order (which can, in extreme cases, provoke rioting, etc.), but on the negotiation of respect for authority in return for fair treatment and officially sanctioned rewards, such as the right to have longer visiting hours. The notion of one side being totally powerful and the other totally powerless is very far from the truth. Therefore, to return to our first question, we can say that power in language definitely isn't the same as the speech of powerful people, but that *any* speaker can potentially be a powerful speaker in particular contexts and that power is something that speakers negotiate within actual interactions. In this chapter we will look in more detail at the various ways in which speakers learn to do this.

Having drawn even these basic conclusions about the first question, we are now in a better position to consider the second question, *Are there powerful varieties?* We already know, from our discussion of contextual variation in the last chapter, that some varieties, sometimes called *hegemonic* varieties, do indeed exert power over us in the sense that they lay down more or less exactly how we should use English, for example, in a legal contract or during a wedding ceremony. These are indeed 'powerful' varieties in the sense that negotiation is not considered to play a part in them – they simply employ particular established conventions of language use and it is not possible for individuals to ignore those conventions, as doing so would invalidate the performance of speech acts in those varieties. In these situations, however, speakers realise that it is in their interest to conform to the rules, as they want to formalise something they have already decided on or agreed to, be it getting married, the issuing of a writ or the writing of a will. Thus, conforming to strict rules does not simply constrain speakers but also protects them and other participants (e.g. landlord and tenant) equally. Although hegemonic varieties can be challenged, this happens only when a government legitimates change (through new legislation) or when institutions (e.g. the Church) themselves instigate a process of reform relating to the language they use.

The question of whether other varieties are also intrinsically powerful is a more interesting one. Most people would, I think, agree that both politicians and journalists use intrinsically powerful varieties of English in the sense that their language has considerable impact on society and social relations. In this chapter we will discuss political speeches and media English as examples of these varieties, looking at how they both reflect and construct people's perceptions of the world. However, we will also consider whether other, newer, varieties may also be acquiring similar discursive power, including those that might on the surface appear to be concerned with widening accessibility.

Sociolinguistic approaches to contextual variation in language, as we saw in Chapter 8, relate features of language use to speakers' roles and relationships, to the functions of the interaction, as well as to any communicative or cultural norms that may apply in particular situations. To some extent, such approaches can lead to reasonable assumptions about the likely balance of power between speakers (e.g. in a 'typical' classroom interaction between a teacher and a cooperative class, or a routine consultation in a doctor's surgery). They can also help us understand issues of power or solidarity in interactions involving code-switching or style-shifting, for example, when a group of British Asians might switch from English to Gujerati or when an adult speaker might make use of teenage slang.

9.2   Power in interaction

There are many reasons why speakers can be regarded as more or less powerful participants in conversational interaction. One speaker may simply be more fluent in the language than another, so that a speaker of English as a first language might be expected to have more awareness and control of conversational strategies in the language than a speaker of English as a foreign language. Or the social roles of the speakers may also be unequal, so that one speaker might be regarded as having more status and authority than the others and be given more speaking opportunities, interrupted less, and so on. In some cultures, factors such as respect for the speech of older people or self-consciousness about using a non-standard dialect might also come into play, altering power relations between conversational partners and again allowing some speakers to have longer turns and more control over how the conversation progresses. Or one conversational partner may just happen to know more about the topic of conversation than the others and therefore be, temporarily at least, 'given the floor'. Issues concerning the identity of the participants, their social and cultural background, their knowledge or expertise inevitably have to be taken into account when we analyse particular interactions.

One area in which issues of power can be seen in interaction is in the way speakers of different regional and social backgrounds, when talking to each other, sometimes try to change their speech patterns (particularly their accents) in order to sound more, or less, like their conversational partners. When they want to sound more alike, this process of adjustment is called 'convergence'. However, if speakers wish to maintain unequal power relations and to keep their distance, they will instead 'diverge', making their own accents even more marked. The decision to converge or diverge is not always a conscious one and sometimes speakers can be surprised at the way their own accents 'accommodate' to those of others, feeling that they have no conscious control over the phenomenon. Whether consciously performed or not, however, speakers' convergence or divergence is frequently connected with the influence of social status, fashion and so on. For example, today in Britain the increasingly widespread accent known as *Estuary English* is thought by many linguists to have come about through a process of convergence between Cockney and RP accents encouraged by the economic power of the 'yuppie' or entrepreneurial class associated with London in the 1980s. In 1998 the Prime Minister Tony Blair appeared on a TV chat show hosted by the entertainer Des O'Connor, who has a fairly broad London accent, and was heard to 'converge' quite noticeably with his host by dropping some of his aitches and using glottal stops in words such as *little* and *put*. A *Times* newspaper story on the topic carried the headline 'Cockney Blair drops in but leaves 'is aitches behind' and reported that, although Downing Street had denied that the Prime Minister had 'modulated his normally cultured tones' deliberately for the show, an analysis of the interview 'showed that he strayed into Estuary English'.[1] Clearly, the story was thought newsworthy, as traditionally British Prime Ministers have tended to be associated with upper-class or educated regional accents. Because the Cockney accent has frequently been stigmatised for its association with London's East End, 'Estuary' is itself sometimes stigmatised as an accent used to widen popular appeal at the expense of 'standards'.

One of the most interesting things about convergence with regard to the issue of power, however, is that while a decision to converge might be viewed as showing anxiety about not being accepted by a certain addressee or audience (therefore showing 'weakness'), it might also be a more controlled and even manipulative strategy for gaining, ultimately, greater power. A Prime Minister changing his accent to appeal more to a popular chat show audience might seem to be too concerned about his street credibility, yet at the same time he is avoiding giving the impression of haughty detachment, or of hiding behind the privilege of high office. His informality and flexibility come to the fore, and he sounds like 'one of us', which is just what he needs to strengthen his appeal to the ordinary voter.

9.3 Powerful varieties

Some varieties are associated with power by virtue of their important influence in society. A measure of the extent of their power is the frequency with

---

[1] Andrew Pierce, 'Cockney Blair drops in but leaves 'is aitches behind', *The Times*, 4 June 1998.

which people make complaints about them, drawing attention to the kind of language typically associated with these varieties and attempting to expose the ways in which they trick or deceive the public, evade important matters, complicate what should be expressed more clearly, and so on. There have been several high-profile campaigns to draw public attention to the way jargon is used by people in power to deceive, confuse or mislead. In the US in the 1970s the National Council of Teachers of English formed a 'Committee on Public Doublespeak', establishing a system of 'awards' to expose the principal culprits in semantic distortion, propaganda and language designed to misrepresent. In 1979 the Committee gave the nuclear power industry an award for euphemistic language used in connection with the incident at Three Mile Island, when, for example, a nuclear reactor accident was referred to as a 'normal aberration' and plutonium contamination was called 'infiltration'.[2] Despite the considerable success that such campaigning has had on the way official documents for the public are written and designed, it would be dangerous to assume that the use of a more accessible style necessarily makes powerful domains more accountable and therefore less powerful. While plainer words are easier to understand than jargon, they too can be used in subtle ways to hide the truth and camouflage responsibility. And the growing trend in the media towards audience participation programmes and live studio debates with politicians cannot guarantee that discursive power has shifted in favour of the general public. During the General Election campaign in Britain in 2001 many ordinary voters complained that the politicians did not engage in any genuine exchanges with them at all, but merely spoke to carefully chosen supporters in stage-managed settings. Some individuals and groups were so convinced that campaigning politicians did not want to talk to them spontaneously that they began to heckle, throw missiles and generally disrupt the election campaign at every opportunity. Others, who did manage to initiate a direct verbal exchange, showed their scepticism by refusing to accept politicians' words, however straightforward, as genuinely meant. A woman who confronted Tony Blair face to face about unacceptable delays in the medical treatment of her partner, a cancer patient at a hospital that the Prime Minister was about to visit, refused to accept as truthful his reply that he was 'sorry' about the situation she described. She simply retorted, 'No, you're not sorry', refusing absolutely to allow his sympathetic words to pacify her. By reacting in this way the woman was signalling that she did not believe

---

[2] They also introduced 'The Orwell Awards' to recognise works that had made an outstanding contribution to the critical analysis of public discourse, for example Dwight Bolinger's book, *Language, the Loaded Weapon* (1980). An equally successful campaign based in Britain, the *Plain English Campaign*, also introduced an award system: 'The Golden Bull Awards', to publicise and ridicule unclear English, and 'The Crystal Mark', to reward a high standard of clarity in language and layout on leaflets, brochures, forms, instructions, etc.

a politician could ever actually engage in 'natural' and honest interaction with an ordinary member of the public.

9.3.1 The English of politicians

Whatever the general public think of their efforts, politicians today are anxious to speak in a language accessible to ordinary people. However, the process of change in their speech has been a gradual one, paralleling changes in society, particularly (with regard to Britain) the change towards a less deferential attitude to those in positions of power and influence. In an essay called 'Propaganda and Demotic Speech' written in 1944, George Orwell complained about the 'remoteness' of politicians from the public and that 'clear, popular, everyday language seems to be instinctively avoided'. He argued that broadcast speeches and news bulletins at the time failed to make any impression on 'the average listener, because they are uttered in stilted bookish language and, incidentally, in an upper-class accent'. Orwell advocated that speech writers should study transcriptions of spontaneous speech in order to make their written English 'more essentially speakable'. He looked forward to a time when the country might have 'a genuinely democratic government . . . which will want to tell people what is happening . . .', adding that such a government 'will need the mechanisms for doing so, of which the first are the right words, the right tone of voice'.[3]

Today Orwell's hopes seem somewhat naive, however significant they were at the time. The majority of Britain's politicians are today highly conscious of the importance of choosing the 'right words' and speaking with the 'right tone of voice'. However, the problem now is that the words and the way they are delivered have come increasingly under the control of media-conscious and often media-trained speech writers and advisers. While political *spin* is not an exclusively modern phenomenon, today's *spin doctors* manipulate a media machine of unprecedented speed and sophistication to help politicians put a favourable slant on potentially unpopular policies or attempt damage limitation when something goes wrong. Ironically, political parties spend as much time trying to expose the spin in the language of their opponents as they do trying to conceal it in their own. An example from the 2001 British General Election campaign was the use by the Conservative Party of the phrase *secure reception centres* to refer to the places where they proposed detaining all asylum seekers while their application for asylum was being processed. On the other hand, their opponents in the Labour Party and elsewhere had taken to referring to these same places as *prisons* and *boot camps*.

---

[3] Sonia Orwell and Ian Angus (eds), 1968 *The Collected Essays, Journalism and Letters of George Orwell*, vol III, 'As I Please 1943–1945'. London: Secker and Warburg.

The tendency for politicians to use bland or euphemistic terms is one of the main targets for criticism today. When the US and Britain resorted to attacking areas of Iraq with cruise missiles following Iraq's invasion of Kuwait, Bill Clinton (then US president) and Tony Blair often used sanitised language to describe these attacks. One characteristic of their rhetoric was the use of familiar verbs with new meanings. Typical of this tendency was the use of a verb such as *degrade* in expressions like 'designed to *degrade* Saddam's capacity to develop and deliver weapons of mass destruction', or 'our aim is to *degrade* his ability to threaten his neighbours'. Here, *degrade* was used to mean something like *reduce in strength*, but the public could not possibly know exactly what was intended – whether this implied *get rid of completely*, for example. And many other expressions have since then been routinely used to avoid the blunt admission of tragic wartime blunders, such as *collateral damage* for the killing and maiming of civilians near the target area, or *friendly fire* for accidental attacks on allied forces.

It is not just in times of international conflict that the English of political leaders has been lamented. In an article published in *The Guardian* in 2001 John Sutherland attacked the demise of words once used to signify genuine public good and now reduced in resonance or contaminated by negative associations. Today a word like *service* tends to bring to mind *service sector* (rather than service to the community, for example); *benefit* calls up associations of monetary handouts, and *asylum*, through conjunction with *bogus*, is losing its meaning of 'safe place of refuge'. Sutherland also sees 'an ideology of nervousness' in the 'core rhetoric' of today's politicians, leading them to avoid committing themselves to any action beyond saying, for example, that they will *address* a problem (which really means no more than to inspect it). Sutherland concludes:

> The present custodians of the common good, in their linguistic soul, see themselves as doing or making nothing. They merely 'deliver' (or 'roll out', as one might lay a carpet) what, by implication, others have done or made. They aspire no higher than to be a kind of service provider or political parcel force: getting the goods (common or otherwise) from there to here.
>
> (John Sutherland, 'How the potent language of civic life was undermined', *The Guardian*, 20 March 2001)

9.3.2 Media English

The media, whether we mean the press, TV or radio broadcasting (not forgetting the Internet as a medium for news and current affairs), represent the most dominant channels through which we receive information about the world, people and events. Media English, however, does not communicate its content to us without at the same time influencing the ways in which we perceive that content. Indeed, the language used by the media tends to be the dominant language available to us to describe particular people and events. The media sustain a particular representation and keep it at the forefront of people's minds, so that it is often difficult to think of certain figures (political leaders, pop stars, etc.) without recalling phrases from media accounts of them. Once a particular media representation of a person really takes hold, it becomes a norm for subsequent representations, with journalists often drawing on this established construct as a filter for every new report. Left-wing and liberal media treatment of Margaret Thatcher, British Conservative Prime Minister from 1979 to 1990 and now Baroness Thatcher, is an example of this. While still in office, Thatcher was frequently described as the 'Iron Lady' and indeed she would herself often encourage the media in this kind of representation of her by inventing (or having invented for her) memorable phrases of her own.[4] Since her retirement from political office, this image of Margaret Thatcher has often been revived in media reports of her various speeches and guest appearances in front of the party faithful. One such appearance took place in the British Election campaign of 2001, when Thatcher gave a speech in Plymouth, Devon, ostensibly to rally support for the then leader of the Conservative Party, William Hague, in the run-up to polling day. During the speech, Thatcher gave her audience an assurance that, if it were up to her, she would 'never' allow the British pound to be given up in favour of the euro. This statement showed Thatcher to be somewhat out of line with the official pre-election policy of the Conservative Party on whether Britain should join the European Exchange Rate Mechanism (ERM), which was to rule out joining for the duration of the next parliament (but, by implication, not necessarily for ever). It was, therefore, an easy matter for the anti-Conservative press to present Thatcher's appearance as a significant handicap, rather than a boost, to her party, which would open up old splits between its Euro-friendly and Euro-sceptic factions. Journalists went out of their way to exaggerate Thatcher's strength and Hague's helplessness in the shadow of a former and more charismatic leader of the party. In this extract from a front page report by Will Self in *The Independent* the proverbial strength of Thatcher is in fact developed into a new representation of her, this time a construction perhaps more in keeping with her older age and fame as the party's greatest leader in modern times: that of a magus[5] or priest with magical powers:

Brave Billie watches as the Magus weaves her strange spell

NEVER BEFORE has the future appeared so dated and, by the same token, never before has the past seemed so undeniably up to date. After a lacklustre day of campaigning across the blue remembered hills of the south west, the

---

[4] For example, Thatcher once used the expression 'The Lady's not for turning' to reinforce her resolute stand on a particular issue, adapting the title of a play by Christopher Fry, *The Lady's not for Burning* (1948).

[5] A magus is, more specifically, a priest in the ancient Persian religion of Zoroastrianism.

Arthurian legend that is the Hague bid for the premiership descended at last to the cavernous Pavilion in Plymouth, wherein Margaret Le Fay slept the immemorial sleep of the just. Could brave Billie awake the magician? Could the magician in turn awake that slumbering dragon, the party faithful which, like some dragon couchant, has heretofore seemed less like a fighting phalanx of fanatics than a mere mythical beast of heraldry: crossed blue rinses, with rampant pound signs [. . .]

There she is, small but erect, in a beautifully cut Paisley-patterned blue coat dress. Her hair is that aureole of a ginger-blonde coif that makes her reminiscent of an old print you once saw of the Virgin Queen. Rock on.

The Magus gains the podium and, her impressive embonpoint shielded by a triangle of perspex inscribed with 'Common Sense', she begins to work her strange spell.

(Will Self, *The Independent*, 23 May 2001)

By calling up images of the Arthurian legend and adopting a style reminiscent of epic romance, Self portrays the Conservatives as tied to the past and to their own adulation of their former leader who they believe has special powers capable of reviving their spirits. William Hague becomes 'brave Billie' whose campaign so far has been 'lacklustre' and who turns, in a constituency once securely Conservative but now largely lost to Liberal Democrats and Labour, 'at last' to his more powerful mentor for inspiration. The problem is that he may not be able to 'wake' her, and even she herself may not awaken the party as hoped. And the party, too, is a shadow of its former self, its core supporters ageing traditionalists obsessed with their struggle to keep the pound. Of course, Thatcher still commands respectful attention: she is 'small but erect', smartly dressed and recalls Queen Elizabeth I, a monarch capable of appealing effectively to her subjects through her speeches. However, overall, there are weaknesses under the surface: the analogy with the 'Virgin Queen' implies she is wedded only to her party, much as Elizabeth chose to be, metaphorically, wedded only to England. Physical frailty is suggested by 'she gains the podium', but once there, she does not deliver a merely limited, 'common sense' message; she 'begins to work her strange spell', rousing the audience from their slumber with unmistakable echoes of the heady days of her leadership. The tone of the report is heavily ironic and mocking, however, as shown by 'blue remembered hills' and 'Rock on'. Clearly, Self is writing not in admiration, but in amused and scornful disbelief.

This report is an example of how the English used in newspapers can exert a powerful influence on how we interpret people and events. It is, more specifically, an example of how the *words* chosen by the reporter (writing in this case for broadsheet readers assumed to be well educated and appreciative of wit and subtlety) are central in creating a *version* of the events described. By choosing words associated with legend, magicians and secret powers, Self indirectly imposes on our reading of the event a certain set of liberal belief systems and values that are inconsistent with taking the

Conservatives seriously, for instance, or considering their policies to be forward-looking. The more we align ourselves with those systems, the more entertaining we find the report.

Words would appear to be the most important way in which journalists encourage a particular outlook on what they are writing about. However, to leave it at that would be far too simple, since the words that journalists (and the rest of us) use essentially describe various kinds of *processes* (things that people do, say, think, etc.) and the *participants* involved in these processes either directly or indirectly. They also describe when, where and how participants take part in a process, in other words the *circumstances*. Take, for example, the sentence *Billie awoke the magician in the pavilion*:

Participant 1: *Billie* (subject of clause)
Process: *awoke* (predicator)
Participant 2: *the magician* (object/complement)
Circumstances: *in the pavilion* (adverbial)

Now, clearly, Participant 1 differs from Participant 2 in important ways. *Billie* actually performs the action and so is the **actor**, while *the magician* is **affected** by the action. The process that took place was obviously an action or **actional process**, because *Billie* actually did something. However, if the sentence had been *Billie <u>admired</u> the magician*, the process would not have involved action but a **mental process**. Other mental processes covered by this label might be, for example, *think, look at*, or *whisper*, to which we could respectively apply more precise labels (**cognitive, perceptive** and **verbal process**). If we look at the sentence *Billie is brave*, we have a **relational process**, since the verb *be* only 'relates' *Billie* and *brave*. Other verbs that signal a relational process are *seem, appear* and *become*.

Processes can be **transactive** or **non-transactive**. If we take the clause *The magician opened a book*, the action has two participants, the actor (*the magician*) and something affected by the action (*a book*). From the grammatical point of view, the clause is a transitive one, as it employs a transitive verb (a verb that can have a direct object). The proposition or underlying meaning of the clause is therefore transactive. However, in the clause *The magician thought for a moment*, we have only a single participant who is again the actor, but the process of thinking does not affect anything or anyone else and is therefore non-transactive. This time the verb is an intransitive verb, or one that does not have a direct object.

Before moving on to a more typical newspaper report on an event we should note an important point about the description of actional processes. Although these will normally involve more than one participant, the participants may not necessarily be explicitly identified at all times. For example, in *The entrance to the embassy was blocked*, we are not told who did the blocking – was it embassy officials, the police, hostile crowds? Similarly, in *Some supporters went on the rampage after the match*, we can only guesss who and what was affected by their actions – rival fans, passers-by, buildings, parked cars? If we compare this sentence with one in which those affected by the actional processes are actually mentioned, the representation of the actors will seem more critical and condemnatory: *Some football supporters looted shops, overturned cars and threatened onlookers after the match.* Once we are explicitly told that shopkeepers and innocent people have been affected, we are more likely to be persuaded that the supporters should, for instance, have their passports confiscated or be imprisoned without trial in another country. Because of the emphasis on the affected participants, the question of the civil liberties of the 'actors' is likely to be less important to us than our sense of outrage at their criminal acts. Of course, it is sometimes difficult to detect a major polarisation of participants, as in the following extract from a tabloid report on an incident in which the British Deputy Prime Minister John Prescott punched a protester before an election rally in May 2001. Since both the actions of the protester and the response of the Deputy Prime Minister were in their different ways shocking, the main participants appear to be viewed equally as both 'actors' and 'affected' parties:

Prezza hits protester in brawl

JOHN Prescott punched a protester who hurled an egg at him in an astonishing election brawl last night.

He was then pinned flat on his back by the man, surrounded by an angry crowd of farming, fuel and hunting demonstrators.

The extraordinary fracas broke out after the Deputy Premier arrived for a seaside rally.

As he stepped smiling from his battle bus, he was hit by the egg near his face from only a few inches away. Enraged, Mr Prescott landed a left hook on his startled attacker.

The man retaliated by forcing the 63-year-old Cabinet Minister backwards over a two-foot wall, shoving his hand in Mr Prescott's face and grabbing hold of his tie.

Caught off guard, police and aides moved in to separate the men. White-faced with shock, Mr Prescott was then ushered into the rally at Rhyl, north Wales. A 29-year-old man was led away in handcuffs.

Farm labourer Ron Ingram said: 'Somebody threw an egg and Prescott just turned round and thumped him.'

An elderly woman Labour supporter was left in tears. She said: 'This is awful. I've never seen anything like it before.'

A Labour spokesman said: 'Mr Prescott defended himself from attack as anybody would have done in the circumstances.' [. . .]

(Oonagh Blackman and Bob Roberts, *The Mirror*, 17 May 2001)

A totally neutral representation of the incident is not, however, borne out by closer analysis. If we look at the report, first of all, according to its classification of the participants, we find that Prescott is referred to as 'Prezza' (headline), 'John Prescott', 'the Deputy Premier', 'Mr Prescott' (x3) and 'Prescott'. The use of 'Prezza' in the headline makes us think we are about to read a story, not about the actions of a politician, but perhaps a sports personality well known for his laddish image (it recalls the nickname 'Gazza' given to the English footballer Paul Gascoigne, who was notorious for his failure to control his temper, though still adored by his fans). From the beginning, therefore, the Deputy Prime Minister is represented as 'a bit of a lad', despite his high office. When the protester retaliates following the punch, Prescott is described in more sympathetic terms as 'the 63-year-old Cabinet Minister', a figure whose age and position should have, presumably, ensured that he would not be treated in such an undignified way, even if he had 'landed a left hook' on the protester with the skill of a true boxer. The next noticeable shift in classifying the Deputy Prime Minister comes when a member of the crowd of onlookers refers to him, unceremoniously, as simply 'Prescott'. This witness is identified as a 'farm labourer', however, which provides a clue (given the earlier reference to 'angry crowd of farming, fuel and hunting demonstrators') that he is probably no more a supporter of Prescott than the man who threw the egg.

The protester is classified in the report as 'protester' (headline),' 'a protester', 'the man', 'startled attacker', 'the man', 'a 29-year-old man' and 'somebody'. He is also implied as the 'attacker' in the Labour spokesman's words 'defended himself from attack'. Overall, therefore, he is unidentified except as a violent, anonymous individual. Although he is 'startled' by the punch, he is not described as visibly hurt by it.

When we turn to the actional processes in the report, we need to focus not only on the verb phrases (VPs) that represent them but also any nouns or modifiers that may indicate actions, since the *actor–process–affected* relationship does not have to be expressed simply through the Subject – Predicator – Object structure of a clause. For example, in our report, the use of the noun 'brawl' in the headline represents an actional process, as do the nouns 'fracas' and 'attack' in the body of the report. However, our main concern in a report of this kind will naturally be the VPs associated with the two main participants, as well as those describing the response of onlookers and those with more formal roles. The actional, and what we might call the 'reactional', processes attributed to Mr Prescott as actor are as follows:

Actional/reactional process	Affected person
punched	a protester
arrived	–
stepped smiling	–
Enraged	–
landed a left hook	attacker (i.e. the protester)
White-faced with shock	–
turned round and thumped	him (i.e. the protester)

Compare this with the processes attributed to the protester as actor:

Actional/reactional processes	Affected person
hurled an egg	him (Prescott)
pinned flat on his back (by the man)	He (Prescott)
hit by the egg (thrower = protester)	he (Prescott)
retaliated	(Prescott)
forcing . . . backwards	the 63-year-old Cabinet Minister
shoving his hand in . . . face	Mr Prescott
grabbing hold of . . . tie	his (Mr Prescott)

What is immediately noticeable from these tables is that the person affected by the actions of the protester is mentioned far more frequently than the person affected by the actions of Prescott. This may be simply because the person affected by the actions of the protester happens to be a public figure and therefore well known to the readers of the paper. The protestor is not even mentioned by name, which could be for legal reasons. However, does the more frequent mentioning of Prescott suggest that the report has more sympathy for him than for the protester? Overall, it could be said that the Deputy Prime Minister is presented as both victim and attacker, both liked and disliked. However, the report also seems to ridicule him. It also appeared under a set of photographs of the incident with the very large main headline 'He's 2 Jabs' (this played on the phrase 'Two Jags' which was once used disparagingly of Prescott when the press revealed that he had two Jaguar cars at his disposal). And the report itself goes on to sum up the incident as 'the third embarrassment for the Government in one day', mentioning briefly two other incidents (unrelated to Prescott) involving a protester and hecklers.

The newspaper texts we have looked at so far illustrate the power of the media to influence the way we interpret events and the actions of individuals. They are both written texts, however, and broadcast speech plays at least an equally important role in the world of today's media. In the case of news bulletins written to be read aloud we are still dealing with prepared text, but in TV and radio interviews we have partly prepared and partly spontaneous 'conversations' on specific topics, items of news and issues of public interest. The interviewer usually has a set of questions to ask, but may ask more or fewer than planned, or ask the same question many times in different ways, while the interviewee can predict what sorts of questions might be asked and respond to them either cooperatively or not, as the case may be. Both interviewer and interviewee are usually aware that the broadcast interview, as a 'speech event', should be successfully completed (though interviewees have been known to bring interviews to an abrupt end on occasion). The following is an orthographic transcription of part of an interview broadcast on BBC2's *Newsnight* programme on 22 May 2001. It concerns the same topic as the report by Will Self that we looked at earlier, namely the appearance of former British Prime Minister Margaret Thatcher at a Conservative Party rally in Plymouth, Devon. The interviewer is Jeremy Paxman and the interviewee is Andrew Lansley, then a member of the Shadow Cabinet. A key to the symbols in the transcription can be found on in 7.3 above.

JP: when Margaret Thatcher stood up this evening (.) were you under the impression she was going to support party policy ? (.) and if so how embarrassed were you when she *didn't* =

AL: oh I was under the impression that she would support William Hague which indeed she did (.) and gave him a ringing endorsement (.) [I was also entirely→

JP: [but she didn't seem to support your policy on the euro]

AL: ←I was also entirely (.) entirely under the impression that she would condemn er (.) m Mr Blair (.) and the Labour Party which also [she did

JP: [I was talking about your *policy*]

AL: well (.) [yes bu-

JP: [she doesn't support your *policy*]

AL: you were asking me what Margaret Thatcher *said* this evening and you [didn't show

JP: [you w- no I was just asking whether you were under the *impression* that she was going to support party policy =

AL: no (.) Margaret Thatcher came to support William ↓ *Hague* (.) and she came [also to express her views →

JP: [but she (ended up) not supporting his policy]

AL: ←she came also expressing *her views* (.) erm (.) about the Labour Party and the way in which they were not only (.) increasing *taxes* by stealth but also giving away Britain's *sovereignty* by stealth=

JP: when she says I would *never* be prepared to give up our own currency (.) which is ↑ *not* your party policy (.) your party policy is (.) merely for the next er term of the next er parliament (.) will you discipline any candidate who agrees with her?

AL: no (.) the point (.) we've made it very clear (.) indeed I'm sure you've asked us this question before (.) Margaret Thatcher said exactly the same thing in an article in The Daily Mail this morning (.) the (.) the (.) p policy of the ↓ *party* is very clear (.) it was agreed by the membership endorsed by an eighty-five per cent vote in in September 1998, that we will fight the next election committed to keep the pound in the next *parliament* (.)

> now you know perfectly well Jeremy that the way our democracy [works is that →
>
> JP: [but that's not what (xxx)]
>
> AL: ←at each General Election (.) at each General Election a party goes to the country with its manifesto (.) for the subsequent parliament =
>
> JP: do you [imagine that Mrs Thatcher
>
> AL: [all our policies are for the next parliament]
>
> JP: so you imagine that Margaret Thatcher could have gone to the country in a General Election and said (.) I believe in keeping the ↑ Falklands British (.) for the duration of the next ↓ parliament

One of the first things to note about this extract is that both Paxman and Lansley have competing 'agendas' and therefore need to find ways of taking as much control as possible over the way the interview progresses. It is clear from this extract that Paxman is the more persistent of the two, since Lansley in general fails to shift the focus of the talk away from the issue relating to Mrs Thatcher's apparent departure from party policy on the euro. However, having institutional control of the topic, Paxman's role as interviewer is an intrinsically 'powerful' role: he can begin the interview and 'frame' it in ways that will automatically further *Newsnight*'s, rather than Lansley's, agenda. His opening questions are effective in not only forcing Lansley to talk about Mrs Thatcher, but in using *presupposition* (the assumption of presumed knowledge) to give the impression that Mrs Thatcher's speech is problematical to the Conservative Party rather than supportive in its purpose and effect. When Paxman asks 'how embarrassed were you when she didn't' [support party policy], the presupposition is that Lansley was embarrassed to some extent. This opening strategy places Lansley on the defensive immediately, since he has to counteract both the implication that Mrs Thatcher did not support party policy and the assumption that he was embarrassed by her speech. Lansley's adoption of Paxman's own phrase 'under the impression' leads him into some difficulty, as this phrase implies that the impression held was a false one. This is why he quickly uses a relative clause to 'cancel' this possible meaning: 'I was under the impression that she would support William Hague <u>which indeed she did</u> (.) and gave him a ringing endorsement'. Having taken the risk of doing this once, Lansley then does it again, initially suggesting a meaning that he does not actually want to suggest and then having to explicitly cancel it: 'I was also entirely under the impression that she would condemn er (.)m Mr Blair (.) and the Labour Party <u>which also she did</u>'. Paxman's response is to stick to his original focus on Mrs Thatcher's departure from party policy, which Lansley attempts to counteract by inaccurately claiming that he was asked 'what Margaret Thatcher <u>said</u> this evening'.

Paxman simply corrects him on this point, again forcing him back to the very topic he has been trying to evade. Lansley now manages for the first time to attack Labour Party policies, but Paxman ignores this attempt to change topic. He returns to the assumed clash between Mrs Thatcher's own views and party policy, presenting Lansley with a further problem through the question 'will you discipline any candidate who agrees with her?' The implication here is that any candidate agreeing with Mrs Thatcher would automatically be *disagreeing* with party policy and would be liable to disciplinary action. At this point Lansley shows some uncertainty as to how best to respond, as revealed by his false starts and reformulations, but suggests that Mrs Thatcher is not in disagreement with party policy because it is understood that the policy concerns only what happens during the next parliament. He gains some headway in the interview here by adding 'now you know perfectly well Jeremy that the way our democracy works is that . . . at each General Election . . . a party goes to the country with its manifesto (.) for the subsequent parliament'. The ploy 'you know perfectly well' is effective in turning the tables on Paxman, as it suggests that the interviewer is being deliberately stubborn rather than arguing from reasonable assumptions. The use of Paxman's first name reinforces Lansley's advantage, making him seem the less aggressive, more conciliatory speaker. Nevertheless, rather than concede the point made by Lansley, Paxman chooses to ridicule it further by drawing yet more provocative conclusions. The analogy with Thatcher's commitment to keeping the Falkland Islands British negatively implies that the Conservative Party has lost the ability to be resolute and dependable in their policies.

Finally, it is worth noting the turn-taking behaviour in this dialogue. The interviewer tries to control the interaction by repeated interruption (Paxman interrupts Lansley six times but is interrupted only once himself). The interviewee adopts various strategies to keep 'the floor' as well as to 'recover' after any interruptions. For example, Lansley uses clauses linked with 'and' to avoid pausing, extends some sentences by means of relative clauses like 'which indeed she did', and tries not to pause at the end of sentences. To diminish the effect of Paxman's interruptions he tries to resume the grammatical structure and lexis that he is temporarily forced to abandon, as when his 'she came also to express her views' is resumed as 'she came also expressing her views'.

9.3.3 Other powerful varieties

We have already seen that the prerogative of interviewers and questioners to control the way a spoken exchange develops is an important source of power. This kind of control is not limited to media contexts, however, but is becoming increasingly familiar to most of us in our daily lives. The rapid increase in the use of call centres by large companies and organisations is bringing about a significant change in the way we deal with everyday matters such as health, telephone, electricity and other services. Although call centres are intended to make communication with large companies easier, many people find communicating with them stressful and intimidating. Call handlers, too, find their work stressful and have been the victims of 'phone rage' from frustrated callers.

Call centres, in the interest of speeding up their business, attempt to take as much control as possible of the way communications with callers progresses. Once connected, a caller may be asked to choose the service they want by pressing particular numbers or symbols on their phone and it may be some time before they hear a voice that is not recorded. As soon as they are speaking to a call handler, the exchange usually begins with a rapid sequence of predetermined questions about customer reference numbers or other identifying information to enable the call handler to retrieve the relevant data on the computer screen in front of them. Once this has been done, communication may continue to be procedurally controlled, for example, so that the caller gives the necessary information in the order most helpful to the call handler. While the call handler already knows the sequence of questions and answers to be followed and is therefore a powerful speaker, the caller lacks such knowledge and can only react to instructions as they come. To some extent callers may be happy to follow a call handler's lead if this is the quickest way to achieve the purpose of the call (e.g. to book train tickets). However, a caller might also adopt strategies that may not be wholly welcomed by the call handler, such as asking for information to be repeated or for the call handler to speak more slowly or clearly. The caller might also attempt to engage the call handler in a more spontaneous style of talk, but although the call handler might respond favourably to this, the pressure to conclude the call effectively and move on to the next caller will be strong. As calls may be monitored, call handlers avoid departing for too long from the 'script', keeping the pressure on callers to give brief answers and make clear choices and decisions. In a newspaper article attacking the automation and lack of personal response given to callers to the British National Health Service helpline, NHS Direct, Sarah Boseley represented an exchange with a call handler as follows:

'This is NHS Direct. Name please.'
'Oh, hello. I wondered if you could just tell me . . .'
'Postcode?'
'. . . what I should do because my child is in real pain . . .'
'Phone number?'
'. . . with her ears. I've given her the maximum amount of paracetamol it says on the bottle . . .'
'GP's [General Practitioner's] name?'
'. . . but it hasn't helped and all I want to know is . . .'
'Address?'

'...can I give her any more?'

'A nurse will ring you back in half an hour to an hour's time.'

'But she's crying and crying and it's the middle of the night and I want to know what to do RIGHT NOW.'

'She'll ring you back.'

(Sarah Boseley, 'Just hanging on the telephone', copyright Guardian Newspapers Limited 2001)

This is a simulation rather than a transcript of an actual conversation, but its purpose is to show that there was no actual 'conversation' between caller and call handler at all. While the caller uses English normally associated with enquiries and requests for advice and information ('I wondered if you could just...'; 'all I want to know is...'), the call handler merely follows a predetermined set of questions in order to log certain bits of factual information. While these details are of course important (if a nurse is going to ring the caller shortly afterwards), the caller's questions are ignored and conversational cooperation, in its usual meaning, is completely abandoned. Not surprisingly, the caller becomes increasingly frustrated.

Although call centres do not set out to alienate callers (this would obviously mean a loss of business in some cases), they often achieve this result. This may happen because callers, though not totally powerless, *feel* powerless when the person they are speaking to is, to all intents and purposes, trained *not* to allow a natural conversation to develop.

9.4 Summary

We began this chapter by considering how power is best defined in relation to language and whether there are intrinsically powerful varieties. Individual speakers may be powerful for a number of sociolinguistic reasons, but also through the way they use their language in a given context. Certain varieties may be regarded as intrinsically powerful, such as the language of politicians and the media, whether we are concerned with the written or spoken mode. In cases where one speaker has the right to control the framework of an exchange, as in media interviews, this speaker could be said to have a special advantage. Finally, even varieties ostensibly intended to facilitate communication, for example between large organisations and the public, retain power in the sense that they control the technologies used, as well as the interactional choices we may be given.

Activities

1. Find two newspaper reports on the same incident. How are the *actors* and *actional processes* described in each, and how is this likely to affect

the way we might interpret the events reported? What other stylistic factors may be relevant to a comparison between the two texts?

2. Record and transcribe part of a radio or TV interview with a politician or other important figure (e.g. leader of an environmental organisation or trade union representative). Note what strategies the interviewer and interviewee use to fulfil their separate aims. Does one or the other become clearly dominant in controlling the exchange, or does 'power' fluctuate between the two?

Further Reading

See Fairclough (1989) and (1995) for a critical linguistic perspective on how language maintains and changes power relations in society and of ways of analysing these processes. Sarangi and Slembrouck (1996) investigate discursive practices related to power and control in administrative and public service domains. Cameron (2000) includes an investigation of talk in the workplace, particularly call centres. See Beard (1999) for an exploration of the language of politics, including how politicians answer questions in the media and in parliament. See Jaworski and Coupland (1999) for a range of investigative studies of discourse and power in diverse settings.

Chapter 10

The Future of English as an International Language

10.1 Introduction

In Chapter 4 we looked at varieties of English used in an Inner, Outer and Expanding Circle territory (the US, South Asia and Japan respectively), considering some of the distinctive features of these varieties and attitudes towards them. Kachru's three circles model has the advantage of representing reasonably clearly the way English has spread in these different areas: in the Inner Circle largely through migration of English speakers; in the Outer Circle largely through colonisation by English-speaking nations and in the Expanding Circle through foreign language teaching. However, a drawback of the model is that it takes no account of the shifting status of English in many countries of the Expanding Circle. Graddol (1997) points out that in countries like Argentina, Belgium, Denmark, Ethiopia, Lebanon, the Netherlands, Norway, Sweden, and the United Arab Emirates many people now use English as a medium of communication within the country as well as for international communication, so that it is more like a second than a foreign language to them. Of course, unlike the Outer Circle, the Expanding Circle does not at this stage have its own 'institutionalised' varieties of English, though, as we shall see later in this chapter, efforts are already being made in Europe to produce corpora of English as a lingua franca (ELF) which could ultimately lead to the codification and acceptance of features traditionally stigmatised as learner 'errors'. In other words, the 'norm-developing' characteristic applied by Kachru to Outer Circle territories could soon become applicable to the Expanding Circle. These territories have traditionally looked to the Inner Circle for their models of pronunciation and grammar, etc. and have therefore been described by Kachru as 'norm-dependent'.

In attempting to predict the future of English as an international language we need to start with a few statistics. Graddol (1999:62) has predicted that

> ... the number of people using English as their second language will grow from 235 million to around 462 million during the next 50 years. This indicates

that the balance between L1 and L2 speakers will critically change, with L2 speakers eventually overtaking L1 speakers.

On the face of it, such a shift might not appear to augur well for English as a lingua franca, since L2 (that is, English used as a second language) varieties might be expected to overwhelm or destabilise any international variety, leading to a general fragmentation of the language. And this would seem to be particularly likely in places where distinctive nativised or hybrid varieties of English have developed and are routinely used by educated people in their own regional and cultural context. The following recorded dialogue is an example of nativised Malaysian English. The two female interactants are lawyers in Kuala Lumpur and neither is a native speaker of Malay or English (Chandra is a Tamil and Lee Lian is Chinese):

CHANDRA: Lee Lian, you were saying you wanted to go shopping, nak perga tak? [Malay: 'Want to go, not?']
LEE LIAN: Okay, okay, at about twelve, can or not?
CHANDRA: Can lah*, no problem one! My case going to be adjourned anyway.
LEE LIAN: What you looking for? Furnitures or kitchenwares? You were saying, that day, you wanted to beli some barang-barang [Malay: 'buy . . . things']
CHANDRA: Yes lah! Might as well go window-shopping a bit at least. No chance to ronda [Malay: 'patrol, loaf'] otherwise. My husband, he got no patience one!

* lah: an informality/solidarity marker

(From Baskaran (1994). Text reprinted in McArthur, 1998:11)

This variety is characterised by non-standard grammatical forms such as *can or not?*, *He got no patience one* and *furnitures*, as well as borrowings of words and phrases from Malay, like *lah* and *nak perga tak*. McArthur (1998) describes this sample as being 'at an acrolectal level' (i.e. it is the more prestigious form of the variety) with the result that, despite the mixing, it is still roughly comprehensible to people who know English but not Malay, whereas a basilectal form at the lower end of the dialect continuum would not be, despite the frequency of words from English.[1] What is interesting about nativised spoken varieties, therefore, is that they are not in any way fixed or stable but operate along a scale of intelligibility to the rest of the English-speaking world.

[1] McKay (2002:55) notes, with reference to Singaporean English or *Singlish*, that '. . . in some instances, the non-standard variety is in fact used by speakers of the socially dominant group as well as speakers of lower social status, but the former generally only use it in informal contexts to signal social identity and rapport'.

Is English as an international language (EIL) likely, then, to be undermined by the strength and vibrancy of nativised varieties of this kind? This is improbable, because a truly global language evolves to fulfil specific international functions in different parts of the world and is sustained by these functions. It is also sustained by the fact that large numbers of people across the world need to learn EIL, even if they already speak a local variety of English and one or more other languages, like the two Malaysian lawyers above. Brutt-Griffler (2002) has argued that the development of a global language has four 'central features': first, its 'econocultural functions' as a product of a world market and of global science, technology, culture and media; second, its 'stabilization of bilingualism' through the fact that it coexists with local languages in bilingual/multilingual contexts; third, its 'transcendence of the role of an elite lingua franca' (since a global language is learnt by various socio-economic groups, not just an elite); and fourth, the fact that it spreads because many people in a speech community learn it and not because speakers of English migrate to other areas.

In this chapter we will look in more detail at English as an international language, at some of the results of work done to describe it, and at some of the implications (for both spoken and written English) of using new corpora of English as a lingua franca to inform ELT provision. We will also consider whether the future of EIL could be impeded or threatened on the basis of current events and attitudes.

10.2 (Spoken) English as an international language

Crystal (1999) anticipates the emergence of what he terms a World Standard Spoken English (WSSE), which he describes as a 'regionally neutral international spoken standard, acting as a stabilising force on global spoken diversity' (reprinted in Burns and Coffin, 2001:58). Crystal argues that this will be used for international communication in a multi-dialectal world in which many users of English will have three dialects at their disposal, two of them having 'status as educated standards'. There will be one language or dialect marking local identity, a second acting as the educated standard dialect for national communication and marking national identity, and a third dialect (WSSE) acting as the standard for international communication.

How persuasive is this scenario? It might be difficult at this stage to imagine EIL becoming 'regionally neutral' to the point, say, of losing its American or British English characteristics, but it is surely not unreasonable to predict that, as a spoken standard, it will need to be more flexible and responsive to the diversity of international spoken English. There is already ample evidence that English has begun to evolve special characteristics in response to the needs of speakers in multinational and multilingual settings. In the EU in Brussels, for example, speakers of French, German, Greek, Italian and other languages all use English routinely as a common language for communication. In practice, what happens in such a situation is that there is what Crystal refers to as 'the usual sociolinguistic accommodation' resulting in the following:

> . . . a novel variety of 'Euro-English' – a term which has been used for over a decade with reference to the distinctive vocabulary of the Union [. . .], but which must now be extended to include the various hybrid accents, grammatical constructions, and discourse patterns encountered there (ibid:57).

The features of this variety appear to include the influence of a syllable-timed rhythm, the use of simple sentence structure and avoidance of idiomatic and colloquial English. Crystal reports that even British first-language speakers of English working in Brussels told him how they 'felt their own English being pulled in the direction of these foreign-language patterns' and realised they were themselves unconsciously accommodating to a continental European variety of English. This kind of accommodation therefore applies to *all* users of English as a lingua franca, not just to non-native speakers of English, and thus reinforces the argument that EIL does not automatically adopt L1 speakers' norms over those of speakers of other languages.

10.2.1 Towards descriptions of EIL

While Kachru's three circles model of global English takes account of the ever-widening use of English in the Expanding Circle, some applied linguists argue that it neglects the true nature and functions of EIL in these areas. Seidlhofer writes:

> The problem is that since the whole model is historical and geographical, but not really sociolinguistic, it is not designed to deal with the characteristic functioning of the language in the Expanding Circle, as a lingua franca. What Inner and Outer Circle have in common is that in both speakers are using English essentially as an intracommunity language, culturally intrinsic to their society and so necessarily involving matters of social identity [. . .]. But the lingua franca in the Expanding Circle is a totally different situation – it is essentially culturally extrinsic, and the very point is that it does not belong to anybody in particular [. . .].

> (Seidlhofer, 2002a:202–203)

EIL is still at a relatively early stage in its evolution, though recent studies have shown that it is developing its own characteristics. Jenkins (2000) investigated what she termed 'interlanguage talk' (interactions between 'non-native' speakers), establishing which phonological features threatened mutual intelligibility and proposing that these should constitute a phonological 'Lingua Franca Core' and be the essential focus of pronunciation teaching. Features that did not seem to impede mutual intelligibility were then designated 'non-core', even if they were traditionally central to EFL teaching, such as the 'th-sounds' /θ/ and /ð/ , the 'dark l' allophone /ɫ/ found at the end of a word like *cool*, and features like weak forms and stress-timed rhythm. In Jenkins's data, for instance, /θ/ and /ð/ were frequently substituted by other sounds such as /f, v/ or /t, d/ or /s, z/ . Such substitutions can also be found in some L1 varieties of English, so similar instances in EIL should not, according to Jenkins, be treated as targets for remedial pronunciation training (although she acknowledges that some substitutions can be stigmatised in Inner Circle contexts, as in the Cockney pronunciation of *brother* as /brʌvə/). Of course, Jenkins freely admits that there are, and always will be, learners who want to make the effort to acquire 'native-like' pronunciation (even if relatively few actually achieve their goal), but suggests that these are diminishing in number as the majority of users of EIL need the language for communication, not with native speakers but with other users of EIL in multilingual and multicultural contexts. In such contexts, the important thing is to ensure mutual intelligibility, not strict adherence to British RP or General American norms. It is therefore the core features, those which research indicates are central to EIL intelligibility, that Jenkins proposes should be given priority in the classroom.[2]

The interesting thing about these findings is that, when they are considered in the context of the learning and teaching of English worldwide, it is clear that a great deal of time and effort is usually dedicated to non-core items, such as the pronunciation of words with *th*, word stress, or words with strong and weak forms. The focus on non-core items is, of course, to be expected when formal assessment of learners in many countries, especially European countries, has traditionally taken as its model the English of native speakers.

While Jenkins's work has focused on phonology, research by Barbara Seidlhofer has begun to produce a more general description of EIL features. Seidlhofer is compiling a corpus of interactions in English among reasonably fluent speakers from a variety of first-language backgrounds, concentrating on lexico-grammar and discourse.[3] She is interested in identifying, despite

---

[2] Of course, it is not a simple matter to define 'intelligibility'. In its narrowest sense it means word-level recognition of a language, but it also encompasses the broader notions of 'comprehensibility' (the meaning of the text is clear) and 'interpretability' (its intent or purpose can be understood).

[3] The corpus is known as *VOICE*, standing for the Vienna-Oxford International Corpus of English (the project being supported in its initial phase by Oxford University Press). The interactions collected, which include one-to-one interviews, group and private discussions and casual conversation, have been taking place in Vienna, in environments in which English is not the predominant language and where native speakers of English are not involved.

the different first-language backgrounds of her subjects, how far they rely on particular kinds of grammatical construction and lexical choices in EIL interactions and what aspects could be said to lead to either communication success or breakdown. She is also investigating whether some items considered ungrammatical in Standard L1 English are unproblematic and even systematic in EIL. Indeed, Seidlhofer's preliminary findings appear to show that predictable learner 'errors' to which teachers would normally give much time and attention (e.g. failing to use 'correct' forms in question tags; 'omitting' definite and indefinite articles; 'confusing' the relative pronouns *who* and *which*) are not in fact stumbling blocks to intelligibility in EIL. What is more problematical is the asymmetrical use of idiomatic speech, including metaphorical expressions, idioms, phrasal verbs and fixed expressions. Seidlhofer illustrates this very aptly with an example from her fieldnotes:

> In April 2000, I was involved in the following dinner conversation in southern Crete. On my left sat my English (native speaker) friend Peter; on my right, three Norwegians, users of ELF. Yiannis, the Greek waiter (and another ELF speaker) whom we know quite well, appears with several glasses of the local raki, usually complimentary after a meal, and serves it in small glasses to the Norwegians with the words 'this is from the house' (maybe trying to use a phrase that Peter has taught him, but not quite getting it right). The Norwegian woman on my right, Leila, says 'ja ja', nodding to Yiannis. Her response sounds like an acknowledgement that she has received some information, maybe something like 'this is the house raki, we make it', but not thanking. So my English friend Peter and I simultaneously turn to Leila to explain. Peter: 'Yiannis meant that this is ON the house'. But from Leila's facial expression it is clear that she does not know this phrase. So I rephrase saying 'Yiannis meant that it is a PRESENT from them', upon which Leila says 'Ahh!!' and, realizing that she should have thanked Yiannis, looks round to see whether he is still within earshot.
>
> So much for native speaker idiomaticity and its usefulness for ELF.
>
> (Seidlhofer, 2002a:211–212)

An important aim of the work being done on describing EIL is to challenge outdated attitudes towards different users of English. The relevance of native-speaker norms is being debated as never before; indeed native speakers are now being told that they too will have to learn EIL in order to communicate more effectively in international contexts:

> For centuries, 'NSs' have assumed that it is the job of the others, the 'NNSs', to make their English intelligible to NSs. There has never been any question of the opposite scenario. And this situation still obtains in the minds of the vast majority of British and American teachers of English [. . .] The perhaps unpalatable truth for 'NSs' is that if they wish to participate in international communication in the 21st Century, they too will have to learn EIL.
>
> (Jenkins, 2000:227)

The changing perspective on native-speaker varieties of English is reflected in a recent model of EIL developed by Modiano (1999) which places the core features of EIL, and not those of any major variety of English, in the centre. While this model represents an interesting alternative to Kachru's three circles model, it is not uncontroversial. A fuller account of it can be found in Jenkins (2003).

10.2.2 Codification

New corpora of EIL interactions are likely to be of major interest to publishers of learners' dictionaries and English language course books. If particular usages are shown to be widely used and understood by competent non-native speakers from a variety of language backgrounds, these could eventually be referred to as valid alternatives to native-speaker norms. In a discussion paper commissioned by the Language Policy Division of the Council of Europe, Seidlhofer (2002b) recognises the importance in this regard of an eventual codification of EIL 'with a conceivable ultimate objective of making it a feasible, acceptable and respected alternative to ENL in appropriate contexts of learning and use'. She quotes the following discussion by Bamgbose of the role of codification (in the African context), suggesting that it is also relevant to the recognition and acceptance of EIL in Europe:

> I use codification in the restricted sense of putting the innovation into a written form in a grammar, a lexical or pronouncing dictionary, course books or any other type of reference manual . . . The importance of codification is too obvious to be belaboured . . . one of the major factors militating against the emergence of endonormative standards in non-native Englishes is precisely the dearth of codification. Obviously, once a usage or innovation enters the dictionary as correct and acceptable usage, its status as a regular form is assured.
>
> (Bamgbose, 1998:4)

It may be rather naive to assume that the endorsement in dictionaries of particular usages immediately ensures universal acceptability of those forms. This cannot be taken for granted. For example, the 1961 edition of *Webster's New International Dictionary*, known as *Webster's Third*, sparked a furore over its treatment of informal American English usage and prompted charges of 'permissiveness'. Its critics were appalled, for instance, to find *ain't* included in the dictionary, and they objected to citations taken from popular US culture.

10.3 Standard written English

For Crystal (1999) Standard English today 'is a global reality only with reference to the written language: it might more accurately be called World Standard Printed English (WSPE)'. He notes that WSPE remains much the same across the world and that, 'apart from a few instances of literature and humour involving the representation of regional dialect, and the occasional US/UK spelling variation, WSPE has no regional manifestations'. Given the increasing diversity of spoken English varieties across the world, this may seem a risky statement, but it is true that literate users of English currently have no difficulty in understanding quality English language newspapers wherever they are published in the world, making allowance for a few distinctive features such as the occasional use of words from other languages.

Will the stability of standard written English across the world remain constant, however? In considering this question, it might be helpful to return to the notion of codification for a moment. Clearly, those writing and editing reports in the broadsheet press all over the world are currently using grammatical forms and vocabulary that, by and large, can be considered to be familiar standard forms of English. If, however, these same newspapers began to use regional varieties of English systematically and routinely, and especially if these forms were then codified in new dictionaries and style guides and endorsed by governments and employers, then the continued existence of WSPE could be in question. Of course, this is highly unlikely to happen, not least because of the economic advantages of having an international readership, but it would be unwise to discount the possibility altogether. If it did happen, it could lead to far greater regional diversity in all written varieties of English. It might then become necessary to establish the equivalent of a 'lingua franca core' for written as well as spoken English, based on the forms and styles of written English that were found to be most advantageous to writer-reader intelligibility.

10.4 Threats to English

Few people doubt that English, having come this far, will continue to be used as a global language. Certainly the signs are that no other language will replace it in this role in the foreseeable future, though other languages may have increasing influence in trade and communications in particular regions of the world (e.g. Spanish in the Americas). McKay (2002:19) notes several factors that could 'impede' the spread of English, including (a) 'little incentive for individuals, particularly in Expanding Circle countries, to acquire more than a superficial familiarity with the language', (b) the growing pressure on the educational systems of some countries to prioritise the needs of language minority groups, and (c) predictions that the percentage of material stored on the Internet in English may fall from 80 per cent to about 40 per cent of the total information. However, McKay (2002:20) highlights as possibly the most important factor 'resistance to the spread of English arising from negative societal attitudes towards English and English-speaking nations'.

Negative attitudes towards English are likely to increase among organisations opposed to the economic, cultural and military power of the US and its English-speaking allies such as the UK and Australia. The public statements of terrorist groups like al Qaida are not usually delivered in English, as this would be to use the language of the enemy, though English may well play a role as a lingua franca for the promotion of the network's aims and operations in some contexts. Ironically, English could be used to undermine not only Western power but, ultimately, English itself. For if today's most powerful English-speaking nation (the US) were to lose its global influence through the constant need to defend itself from terrorist attack and were to close many of its institutions abroad, etc., the spread of English might become unsustainable. As Crystal (1997:117) writes:

> . . . there is the closest of links between language and power. If anything were to disestablish the military or economic power of the USA, there would be inevitable consequences for the global status of the language. The millions of people learning English in order to have access to this power would begin to look elsewhere, and (assuming the new political magnet used a language other than English) they would quickly acquire new language loyalties.

Could threats also come 'from within'? The vast majority of applied linguists and English language teachers across the world have, in their work, directly or indirectly supported the spread of English while also frequently endorsing language-planning policies aimed at maintaining languages endangered by English. They have welcomed the pluralism and diversity of 'new Englishes' while also arguing the case for international intelligibility and codification. Some, however, see this as an abnegation of responsibility to consider the full cultural and political implications of the spread of English. Pennycook (1995) argues that forms of opposition, which he calls 'counter-discourses', need to be mobilised against the view that assumes the spread of English to be 'natural, neutral and beneficial' when it reproduces inequalities of power and resources in the world. For Pennycook, English language professionals

> . . . should become political actors engaged in a critical pedagogical project to use English to oppose the dominant discourses of the West and to help the articulation of counter-discourses in English.
>
> (Reprinted in Burns and Coffin, 2001:87)

While not every applied linguist or English language teacher would accept Pennycook's analysis here or his suggested solution, many would agree with Graddol that a more ethical and more sensitive approach to the role and nature of ELT in the world will be needed in future, an approach

> . . . which recognises that English is not a universal panacea for social, economic and political ills and that teaching methods and materials, and educational policies, need to be adapted for local contexts. The world is becoming aware of

the fate of endangered languages and more anxious over the long-term impact of English on world cultures, national institutions and local ways of life. Perhaps a combination of circumstances – such as shifting public values, changed economic priorities and regional political expediency – could bring about a serious reversal for British ELT providers at some point in the future. . . .

(Graddol 1997, reprinted in Burns and Coffin, 2001:36)

Any 'serious reversal' of the sort envisaged here would presumably also apply to American ELT providers. However, it could at the same time boost the fortunes of new providers based in the Outer or Expanding Circle, who might be seen as more sensitive to the needs of learners in bilingual or multilingual environments. Thus, the influence of the Inner Circle would wane, but the future of English, in all its international and new varieties, would not itself be threatened.

10.5 Conclusion

In this final chapter we have considered the various trends that indicate how English as an international language or lingua franca may develop in future. One thing is certain: the majority of people using English are already speakers of other languages as well, and bilingualism or multidialectalism are already the norm. The language loyalties of the majority of users of English in future will therefore be divided and, to safeguard their cultural and linguistic identities, some may not wish to use English in situations other than those in which they need to communicate with speakers of other languages. However, as more people begin to use English daily as a second language, it will also continue to be appropriated in ways that suit individual and local contexts and needs, so the future of distinctive varieties of the language is likely to be assured. Given such diversity, it seems safe to predict that those who follow the course of the English language and how it is used will have much to discover, describe and interpret.

Activities

1. Do you think Jenkins (2000) is right to suggest that, for the purposes of pronunciation in EIL, learners should be taught a 'lingua franca core' rather than the traditional range of phonological features based on an Inner Circle model? If this argument were extended to the teaching of vocabulary and grammar, what items do you think might be considered 'core' items for teaching and learning, and which might be 'non-core'?
2. Using the Internet, compare reports from a range of international newspapers in English. What differences, if any, can you find between them in terms of their lexis, grammar and spelling?

Further Reading

For an informative book on the history, cultural foundation, legacy and future of international English, see Crystal (1997) *English as a Global Language*. Graddol (1997) and Graddol and Meinhof (1999) are both important texts in setting out trends and issues related to the use and status of English in the world. Phillipson (1992) analyses the spread of English in relation to the political objectives of English-speaking countries. Both Seidlhofer (2003) and Jenkins (2003) contain analyses of the current debates on English in the global context. See McKay (2002) for a useful exploration of the classroom implications of EIL.

Comments on Activities

Chapter 1

1. In doing this Activity it would be helpful to create network diagrams with lines showing whether each network is 'loose', 'dense' or 'multiplex'. Examples may be found in Wardhaugh (2002:127).
2. In thinking about the 'code-switching' part of this question you might find it helpful to ask friends and relatives what they have observed about the way you use your different languages or dialects.
3. A Standard English version of the first four lines of this verse could read: *I went into a public-house to get a pint of beer, | The publican turns round and says, 'We serve no red-coats here.' | The girls behind the bar could have laughed and giggled themselves to death, | I go out into the street again and say to myself . . . etc.*

   Some of the features of Tommy's dialect are:
   - h-dropping (*be'ind; 'ouse; 'e*)
   - use of a 'double' subject (noun plus pronoun) in *The publican 'e* and *The girls . . . they laughed*
   - non-standard ending on verb in the first person (*I outs into the street*)
   - use of *out* as a verb meaning 'go out'

Chapter 2

1. The following transcriptions are based on Standard Southern British English. Rhotic accents would have an additional consonant in *afford* and *rehearsed*.
   a. speech /spiːtʃ/
   b. plays /pleɪz/
   c. guide /gaɪd/
   d. knee /niː/
   e. afford /əfɔːd/
   f. autumn /ɔːtəm/
   g. rehearsed /rəhɜːst/ or /rɪhɜːst/
2. Patricia Routledge slips into her sensible shoes for another round of amateur sleuthing. A large audience is guaranteed. Tonight's scenario concerns poison pen letters.
   a. round, audience, tonight (or Routledge)
   b. guaranteed
   c. for, of, a

d. poison pen (final /n/ changes to /m/ in anticipation of initial /p/).
   Note also the linking *r* in *for another*

3. a. find (F) + s (I)
   b. melt (F) + ed (I)
   c. combine(F) + ation (D) + s (I)
   d. foot (F) + note (F)
   e. help (F) + less (D) + ness (D)
   f. type (F) + ical (D)
   g. weak (F) + en (D) + ed (I)

4. • whirlwind: compound noun with the structure verb + noun
   • LA : acronym (Los Angeles)
   • snowless: affixation – adjective formed from noun + suffix
   • bureau: borrowed term (from French)
   • gas: clipping (from gasoline)
   • motel: blend of motor + hotel

5. The cohesive ties in this text include:
   Ellipsis:
   Aesthetic [issues], historical [issues], political [issues] and social [issues];
   each [section] concentrating; rudiments of music, [that you] have a reasonable understanding of traditional harmony and [that you] can follow
   a score.
   Reference:
   This course . . . *It* . . . *The* course . . . It;
   Beethoven's music . . . his music . . . its time . . . its style . . . its historical
   significance and influence.
   Substitution:
   Five main sections, *each* . . .
   Lexical links:
   Music . . . rudiments of music . . . harmony . . . score

Chapter 3

1. Words with changed meanings include: *temper* (here 'condition' or
'political climate' of the country); *comfortabell (comfortable* – in the dangerous context, this could mean 'safe'); *ocation (occasion* – here 'opportunity'); *derections (directions* – here 'instructions'); *boy* (here means 'servant');
desire in the everyday sense of 'want'.
   Words no longer in common use: *rogeisch (roguish)* – the word now
occurs most frequently as a noun, e.g. *that boy's a little rogue.*
   Had I not had this ocation . . . , yet I had sent . . .: this structure is not in
use today. In Standard Modern English the main clause of the 'third
conditional' takes a *would + have + past participle* form, so the sentence
would now read: *Had I not had this opportunity to send [a letter] to your
father, I would [still] have sent this boy up to London.*

Use of 'may' in *I desire he may not come downe any more, but that he may be perswaded . . . :* the modal auxiliary 'may' appears to have the force of 'should' here, expressing obligation rather than permission or possibility.

2. While Tess uses Standard English, her mother's speech is represented as regionally and socially marked with dialectal forms such as *zid* for 'saw' and the use of the 'do' auxiliary in positive indicative clauses, such as *she do want 'ee there*. Mrs Durbeyfield presents herself as a source of home-spun wisdom, as reflected in her assertion that those who are born into a business 'know more about it than any 'prentice', dismissing Tess's own statement that she doesn't know that she is skilful or 'apt at tending fowls'. Tess tries to moderate her mother's enthusiasm and excitement by reminding her that she didn't even see Mrs d'Urberville during her stay and that all her son did was call her 'Coz' (from 'Cousin' but also a general term of affection which, as Tess realises, need not have anything to do with his acknowledging her as a relative). Tess expresses her reluctance politely in *I don't altogether think I ought to go* and *I'd rather not tell you why, mother*, while her mother stubbornly insists on her own interpretation of events: *You couldn't expect her to throw her arms round 'ee, an' to kiss and to coll 'ee all at once.* Tess shows her education in noticing that the letter is 'in the third person', and so is not the personal letter that her mother is claiming it is.

3. For example, you could consider two newspaper editorials about war or major national events. Read both texts carefully and list all the features of usage you think are different, grouping them according to whether they are lexical, grammatical or stylistic features.

Chapter 4

1. Books worth consulting for information and data include Crystal (1995, 1997), Jenkins (2003) and McCrum, Cran and MacNeil (1987).
2. Possible fictional texts include: E. M. Forster, *A Passage to India* (1924), Chinua Achebe, *Things Fall Apart* (1958); Rudyard Kipling, *Plain Tales from the Hills* (1888); Toni Morrison, *Beloved* (1987); Ngugi wa Thiong'o, *Secret Lives* (1975), Sam Selvon, *The Lonely Londoners* (1956). Poets include John Agard, Benjamin Zephaniah and Nissim Ezekiel.
3. The journals *World Englishes* and *English Today* are excellent sources of information on the use of English in different countries, both with regard to the description of specific varieties and to relevant attitudes and debates.

Chapter 5

1. Some AAVE features include:
   - spellings 'de' for 'the', 'dey' for 'they', 'dat' for 'that', and 'dem' for 'them', reflecting pronunciation, i.e. /d/ is often used for /ð/

- reduction of word-final clusters in, for example, 'jes' for 'just', 'stan' for 'stand'
- double negative construction in 'When dey <u>ain't no one</u> kin sence it'
- non-rhoticity reflected in spelling, e.g. loss of 'r' in fu' ('for') and yo' ('your') and 'la'ks' ('larks')
- spelling of 'wif' ('with') and 'moufs' ('mouths') shows variant /f/ used for /ð/ in some positions
- non-standard use of possessive pronouns in 'dey'('they') for 'their'
- deletion of first syllable in ''nough' for 'enough'
- use of non-standard subject-verb agreement in 'Robins, la'ks an' all dem things . . . hides'

2. Many poets who use Creole English (e.g. Linton Kwesi Johnson) like to read or 'perform' their work to live audiences. If possible, try to listen to a recording of the poem you choose for this activity.
3. Remember that people can sometimes be self-conscious about their language and may need reassurance about why you wish to ask them questions about it. You will need to devise neutral, non-biased questions to encourage an honest response. For more detailed advice on projects in linguistics see Wray, Trott and Bloomer (1998).

Chapter 6

1. The important thing here is to select a few advertisements from a wide enough range of magazines, e.g. one from a fairly traditional women's magazine, one from a magazine for young men, and one from, say, a health magazine aimed at both women and men.
2. Transcribing even a 20-minute radio talk could take a day – hence the advice to record and transcribe only 'part' of a TV or radio talk, preferably just a few minutes. Since the focus of this question is on speaking turns, interruptions and specific items like the use of hedges and modals by the female speakers, these are the features to concentrate on and to highlight in your transcription.
3. Some possible literary sources for this activity might include the writings of Jane Austen, D. H. Lawrence, Gore Vidal and Jeanette Winterson. An alternative to comparing dialogues might be to compare descriptions of fictional characters. Remember to select extracts that seem to you to be clearly 'gendered', though, either in representing gender normatively or in subverting the norms of gender representation.

Chapter 7

1. Some of the stylistic features you might look out for include the following:

- words used by the joke 'teller' to check that you are listening carefully (e.g. *OK?*)
- possible use by the joke 'writer' of more formal connecting words and phrases (e.g. *however, nevertheless*)
- strategies by both 'teller' and 'writer' to divide their narrative into manageable sections (e.g. *well, now, at this point*)
- other features, such as the use of comments in parentheses by the 'writer' and asides by the 'teller'.
- use of 'fillers' like *er, um, erm* by the 'teller'

2. In representing what people say when they happen to see each other again after many years, this extract does seem to get off to a reasonably credible, if uninspiring, start. The ritualised *well, well, well* and *how nice to see you*, and the rather hackneyed *Doesn't time fly?* all tend to occur in such contexts, where speakers are taken by surprise and fall back on rather conventional ways of dealing with the situation while they activate old memories. The extract also makes use of some grammatical ellipsis, like *Sounds great* and *Too much easy living*, although it is noticeable that there are no total breakdowns in grammatical structure. Karen's *Oh, when was it?* is only a brief interruption of the sentence *I haven't seen you since ... Jane and Dave's wedding*. However, what is most striking about the dialogue, and what distinguishes it most from 'real' speech, is the total absence of non-fluency features. The impression the text gives is of a smooth, continuous interaction with few pauses and no hesitations, false starts or reformulations. Of course, the avoidance of representing non-fluency in texts designed for language learners is predictable. One of the functions of a simulated dialogue like the one above is usually to illustrate specific aspects of English covered in a coursebook unit – here, for example, it could be the use of the past simple for actions at a known point in time, as in *then I came back to Britain*, and the past continuous for actions taking place during a known stretch of time, as in *I was teaching English*. This means that, no matter how naturalistic the simulated dialogue is made to sound, its primary purpose is illustrative.

3. Remember not to reveal the online identities or locations of the people whose online chat or messages you use for this Activity.

Chapter 8

1. You might also like to consider which of the three situations you choose proves easiest to describe by means of the S P E A K I N G model, and the possible reasons for this.

2. *Field*: the text comes from a guidebook for bird-watchers in Europe. Its function is to describe bird species in a concise and systematic way, so as to allow them to be identified with the naked eye or through binoculars. It could be said to belong to the genre of 'descriptive, factual texts for

enthusiasts or experts'. The text identifies itself clearly by means of its main and sub-headings, and includes a great deal of field-specific vocabulary, such as *tapering lower body, Upper-parts golden-buff, sullied grey and finely speckled*, etc.

Tenor: Since the function of this text is simply to inform as quickly as possible (assuming that a birdwatcher might need to refer to it quickly while trying to identify a particular bird) the social roles of the participants are not marked. The text of course assumes that the reader is well informed about birds, and the indicative mood (*Hunting flight [is] usually low*) reflects the information-giving role of the writer. Markers of modality are not present in this text, though *usually* indicates that the owl's hunting flight may not always be low, thus revealing the writer's degree of certainty. Similarly, *Nocturnal but often hunts by day in winter* could be rephrased as *Nocturnal but <u>can be seen</u> hunting by day in winter*.

Mode: This is one entry in a written reference text with a set format. It uses abbreviations (e.g. *Du* for 'Dutch', *Ge* for 'German', *Fr* for 'French', *Sw* for 'Swedish'; *W. and S.* for 'West and South') and refers to other parts of the book by means of *Plate 64* and *Map 191*. Ellipsis is the most noticeable feature of its cohesion (e.g. ellipsis of the grammatical subject in [The bird] *Perches upright . . .* and [it] *Also frequents parks . . .*; ellipsis of pronoun and verb is [Its] *Hunting flight [is] usually low*; ellipsis of article in *as[the] bird looks down*). Frequent prepositional phrases: *with a distinctive . . .*; *with dark eyes*; *with 'knock-kneed' stance*; *with old timber*. Coordinated phrases and clauses are common: [the bird is] *Nocturnal* (clause 1) *but [it] often hunts by day in winter* (clause 2).

3. You might wish to choose one literary text for this Activity. There are countless literary examples of register-mixing, but a poem by Henry Reed (1914–1986) called 'Naming of Parts' (from 'Lessons of the War' in the volume *A Map of Verona*, 1946) has often been used to illustrate this feature. You can also find the poem and a commentary on it in Fowler (1996).

Chapter 9

1. See Chapter 4 of Thomas and Wareing (1999) for further discussion of media language and of sample extracts from newspaper reports.
2. See my warning under Chapter 6 (Qu. 2) above regarding the length of recording.

Chapter 10

1. With regard to possible 'core' and 'non-core' items in lexico-grammar, you could consider where you would, for instance, place the following: 'false friends' like *sensible* and *sensitive*; article use; distinction between

present perfect and past simple; structure of conditional clauses; word order; 'simple' versus 'continuous' aspect; inversion of subject and verb after 'not only . . .'; modal auxiliaries.

2. You should find your own newspaper extracts for this Activity, but for a sample discussion on extracts from two Indian English Language newspapers see Fennell (2001:261–264).

References

Aitchison, J. 1995 *Linguistics: An Introduction* London: Hodder and Stoughton.

Aitchison, J. 1997 *The Language Web: The Power and Problem of Words* Cambridge: Cambridge University Press.

Bakhtin, M. 1981 *The Dialogic Imagination: Four Essays* ed. M. Holquist, trans. C. Emerson and M. Holquist, Austin: University of Texas Press.

Bamgbose, A. 1998 'Torn between the norms: innovations in world Englishes.' *World Englishes* 17/1:1–14.

Barber, C. 1993 *The English Language: A Historical Introduction* Cambridge: Cambridge University Press.

Baron, N.S. 2000 *Alphabet to Email: How Written English Evolved and Where it's Heading* London: Routledge.

Barrell, J. 1983 *English Literature in History 1730–1780: An Equal, Wide Survey* London: Hutchinson.

Bauer, L. 1994 *Watching English Change* London and New York: Longman.

Bauer, L. and Trudgill, P. (eds) 1998 *Language Myths* Harmondsworth: Penguin.

Baugh, A.C. and Cable, T. 2002 *A History of the English Language* Fifth edition. London: Routledge.

Beard, A. 1999 *The Language of Politics* London and New York: Routledge.

Bex, T. and Watts, R.J. (eds) 1999 *Standard English: The Widening Debate* London and New York: Routledge.

Biber, D. 1988 *Variation Across Speech and Writing* Cambridge: Cambridge University Press.

Biber, D. and Finegan, E. (eds) 1994 *Sociolinguistic Perspectives on Register* Oxford: Oxford University Press.

Biber, D., Johansson, S., Leech, G., Conrad, S. and Finegan, E. 1999 *The Longman Grammar of Spoken and Written English* Harlow: Longman.

Block, D. and Cameron, D. (eds) *Globalization and Language Teaching* London and New York: Routledge.

Bolinger, D. 1980 *Language – The Loaded Weapon: The Use and Abuse of Language Today* London and New York: Longman.

Bristow, J. 1997 *Sexuality* London and New York: Routledge.

Brock, M.N. 1991 'The Good Feeling of Fine: English for Ornamental Purposes.' *English Today* 26:51.

Brutt-Griffler, J. 2002 *English as an International Language* Clevedon: Multilingual Matters.

Bryson, B. 1990 *Mother Tongue: The English Language* London: Penguin Books.

Bryson, B. 1994 *Made in America* London: Black Swan, 1998.

Bühler, K. 1934 *Sprachtheorie* Jena: Fischer.

Burnley, D. 2000 *The History of the English Language: A Source Book* Second edition. Harlow: Pearson Education.

Burns, A. and Coffin, C. (eds) 2001 *Analysing English in a Global Context: A Reader* London and New York: Routledge.

References

Burton-Roberts, N.C. 1997 *Analysing Sentences: An Introduction to English Syntax* Second edition. Harlow: Addison Wesley Longman.

Cameron, D. (ed.) 1998 *The Feminist Critique of Language* London: Routledge.

Cameron, D. 2000 *Good to Talk? Living and Working in a Communication Culture* London: Sage.

Cameron, D. and Kulick, D. 2003 *Language and Sexuality* Cambridge: Cambridge University Press.

Carver, C.M. 1987 *American Regional Dialects. A Word Geography* Ann Arbor: University of Michigan Press.

Coates, J. 1996 *Women Talk: Conversation Between Women Friends* Oxford: Blackwell.

Coates, J. and Cameron, D. (eds) 1988 *Women in their Speech Communities: New Perspectives on Language and Sex* London and New York: Longman.

Cornbleet, S. and Carter, R. 2001 *The Language of Speech and Writing* London and New York: Routledge.

Crystal, D. 1984 *Who Cares About English Usage?* Harmondsworth: Penguin.

Crystal, D. 1995 *The Cambridge Encyclopedia of the English Language* Cambridge: Cambridge University Press.

Crystal, D. 1997 *English as a Global Language* Cambridge: Cambridge University Press.

Crystal, D. 1999 'The Future of Englishes.' *English Today* 15/2. Burns and Coffin (op. cit.), 2001:53–64.

Crystal, D. 2001 *Language and the Internet* Cambridge: Cambridge University Press.

DeCamp, D. 1997 'The development of pidgin and creole studies.' In Valdman, A. (ed.) *Pidgin and Creole Linguistics* Bloomington: Indiana University Press: 3–20.

Dobranski, S.B. 1999 *Milton, Authorship and the Book Trade* Cambridge: Cambridge University Press.

Dougill, J. 1987 'English as a decorative language.' *English Today* 12:33.

Eckert, P. and McConnell-Ginet, S. 2003 *Language and Gender* Cambridge: Cambridge University Press.

Edwards, V. 1986 *Language in a Black Community* Clevedon: Multilingual Matters.

Fairclough, N. 1989 *Language and Power* London: Longman.

Fairclough, N. 1995 *Critical Discourse Analysis* London: Longman.

Fennell, B.A. 2001 *A History of English: A Sociolinguistic Approach* Oxford: Blackwell.

Finch, G. 1998 *How to Study Linguistics* Basingstoke: Macmillan.

Fowler, R. 1996 *Linguistic Criticism* Second edition. Oxford: Oxford University Press.

Freeborn, D. 1992 *From Old English to Standard English: A Course Book in Language Variation Across Time* Basingstoke: Macmillan.

Graddol, D. 1997 *The Future of English?* London: British Council. Chapter 5 reprinted in Burns, A. and Coffin, C. (eds) 2001:26–37.

Graddol, D. 1999 'The decline of the native speaker.' *AILA Review* 13:57–68

Graddol, D., Leith, D. and Swan, J. 1996 *English: History, Diversity and Change* London and New York: Routledge.

Graddol, D. and Meinhof, U. (eds) 1999 'English in a Changing World.' *AILA Review* 13.

Gupta, A.F. 1999 'Standard Englishes, Contact Varieties and Singapore Englishes.' In Gnutzmann, C. (ed.) 1999 *Teaching and Learning English as a Global Language: native and non-native perspectives* Tübingen: Stauffenberg Verlag: 59–72.

Halliday, M.A.K. 1973 *Explorations in the Functions of Language* London: Edward Arnold.

Halliday. M.A.K. 1994 *An Introduction to Functional Grammar* Second edition. London: Edward Arnold.

Hartley, L.C. and Preston, D.R. 1999 'The Names of US English: Valley Girl, Cowboy, Yankee, Normal, Nasal and Ignorant.' In Bex, T. and Watts, R.J. (op. cit.) 1999:207–238.

Harvey, K. 2000 'Describing camp talk: language/pragmatics/politics.' *Language and Literature* 9/3:240–260.

Hewitt, R. 1986 *White Talk Black Talk* Cambridge: Cambridge University Press.

Hoffer, B.L. and Honna, N. 1999 'English in Japanese society: reactions and directions.' In Graddol, D. and Meinhof, U. (eds) *AILA Review* 13, 48–56.

Holmes, J. 2001 *An Introduction to Sociolinguistics* Second edition. Harlow: Pearson Education.

Hughes, A. and Trudgill, P. 1996 *English Accents and Dialects* London: Arnold.

Hymes, D. 1972 'On communicative competence.' In Pride, J.B. and Holmes, J. (eds) 1972 *Sociolinguistics: Selected Readings* Harmondsworth: Penguin, 269–293.

Jackson, H. 1989 *Words and Their Meaning* London: Longman.

Jakobson, R. 1960 'Closing statement: linguistics and poetics.' In Sebeok, T.A. (ed.) *Style and Language* Cambridge, Mass.: MIT Press.

Jaworski, A. and Coupland, N. (eds) 1999 *The Discourse Reader* London and New York: Routledge.

Jenkins, J. 2000 *The Phonology of English as an International Language: New Models, New Norms, New Goals* Oxford: Oxford University Press.

Jenkins, J. 2003 *World Englishes: A Resource Book for Students* London and New York: Routledge.

Kachru, B.B. 1983 *The Indianization of English: The English Language in India* Oxford: Oxford University Press.

Kachru, B.B. 1989 'Teaching world Englishes.' *Indian Journal of Applied Linguistics* 15/1:85–95.

Kirkpatrick, A. (ed.) 2002 *Englishes in Asia: Communication, Identity, Power and Education* Melbourne: Language Australia.

Kramsch, C. 1998 *Language and Culture* Oxford: Oxford University Press.

Kubota, R. 2002 'The impact of globalization on language teaching in Japan.' In Block and Cameron (op. cit.) 2002:13–28.

Kurath, H. (ed.) et al 1939–1943 *Linguistic Atlas of New England* (3 vols, in 6 parts) Providence, RI: Brown University Press for the American Council of Learned Studies.

Labov, W. 1966 *The Social Stratification of English in New York City* Washington, DC: Center for Applied Linguistics.

Labov, W. 1972 *Language in the Inner City* Philadelphia: University of Pennsylvania Press.

Lakoff, R. 1975 *Language and Woman's Place* New York: Harper and Row.

Leech, G., Deuchar, M. and Hoogenraad, R. 1982 *English Grammar for Today: A New Introduction* Basingstoke: Macmillan.

Le Page, R. and Tabouret-Keller, A. 1985 *Acts of Identity* London: Cambridge University Press.

Lippi-Green, R. 1997 *English with an Accent* London: Routledge.

Loveday, L.J. 1996 *Language Contact in Japan* London: Oxford University Press.

McArthur, T. 1998 *The English Languages* Cambridge: Cambridge University Press.

McCrum, R., Cran, W. and MacNeil, R. 1987 *The Story of English*. London: Faber and BBC Books.

McKay, S.L. 2002 *Teaching English as an International Language* Oxford: Oxford University Press.

References

Mencken, H.L. 1936 *The American Language* Fourth edition. New York: Knopf.

Milroy, J. and Milroy, L. 1991 *Authority in Language. Investigating Language Prescription and Standardisation* Second edition. London: Routledge and Kegan Paul.

Milroy, L. 1980 *Language and Social Networks* Oxford: Basil Blackwell.

Modiano, M. 1999 'Standard English(es) and educational practices for the world's lingua franca.' *English Today* 15/4:3–13.

O'Grady, W., Dobrovolski, M. and Katamba, F. (eds) 1997 *Contemporary Linguistics: An Introduction* Adapted edition. Harlow: Addison Wesley Longman.

Orwell, G. 1944 'Propaganda and Demotic Speech.' Reprinted in Orwell. S. and Angus, I. (eds) 1968 *The Collected Essays, Journalism and Letters of George Orwell, Vol III: As I Please 1943–1945* London: Secker and Warburg.

Pearsall, J. (ed.) 1998 *The New Oxford Dictionary of English* Oxford: Oxford Univerity Press.

Pennycook, A. 1995 'English in the world/The world in English.' In Tollefson, J.W. (ed.) 1995 *Power and Inequality in Language Education* Cambridge: Cambridge University Press, 34–58.

Phillipson, R. 1992 *Linguistic Imperialism* Oxford: Oxford University Press.

Preisler, B. 1999 'Functions and forms of English in a European EFL country.' In Bex and Watts (op. cit.), 239–267.

Rampton, B. 1995 *Crossing: Language and Ethnicity Among Adolescents* London: Longman.

Roach, P. 2000 *English Phonetivs and Phonology: A Practical Course* Third edition. Cambridge: Cambridge University Press.

Rogers, H. 2000 *The Sounds of Language: An Introduction to Phonetics* Harlow: Pearson Education.

Rooney, K. (Editor-in-Chief) 1999 *Encarta World English Dictionary* London: Bloomsbury.

Rosewarne, D. 1994 'Estuary English: Tomorrow's RP?' *English Today* 10/1:3–8.

Sarangi, S. and Slembrouck, S. 1996 *Language, Bureaucracy and Social Control* Harlow: Addison Wesley Longman.

Sebba, M. 1993 *London Jamaican* London: Longman.

Sebba, M. 1997 *Contact Languages: Pidgins and Creoles* London: Macmillan.

Seidlhofer, B. 2002a '*Habeus corpus* and *divide et impera*: "Global English" and applied linguistics.' In Spelman Miller, K. and Thompson, P. (eds) 2002 *Unity and Diversity in Language Use* London: Continuum.

Seidlhofer, B. 2002b 'A concept of international English and related issues: from "real English" to "realistic English"?' Provisional version. Strasbourg: Language Policy Division of the Council of Europe.

Seidlhofer, B. (ed.) 2003 *Controversies in Applied Linguistics* Oxford: Oxford University Press.

Short, M. 1996 *Exploring the Language of Poems, Plays and Prose* London: Addison Wesley Longman.

Slembrouck, S. 1992 'The parliamentary Hansard "verbatim" report: the written construction of spoken discourse.' *Language and Literature* 1/2:101–119.

Smitherman, G. 1995 'Testifyin, sermonizin, and signifyin: Anita Hill, Clarence Thomas, and the African American Verbal Tradition.' In Smitherman, G. (ed.) *African American Women Speak Out on Anita Hill–Clarence Thomas* Detroit, MI: Wayne State University Press, 224–242.

Smitherman, G. 1999 *Talkin That Talk: Language, Culture and Education in African America* London and New York: Routledge.

Spolsky, B. 1998 *Sociolinguistics* Oxford: Oxford University Press.

Stockwell, P. 2002 *Sociolinguistics: A Resource Book for Students* London: Routledge.

Tannen, D. 1990 *You Just Don't Understand: Women and Men in Conversation* New York: William Morrow.

Thomas, L. and Wareing, S. (eds) 1999 *Language, Society and Power: An Introduction* London and New York: Routledge.

Thorne, S. 1997 *Mastering Advanced English Language* Basingstoke: Macmillan.

Tottie, G. 2002 *An Introduction to American English* Oxford: Blackwell.

Trudgill, P. 1972 'Sex, covert prestige, and linguistic change in the urban British English of Norwich.' *Language in Society* 1:179–195.

Trudgill, P. 1999 *The Dialects of England* Second edition. Oxford: Blackwell.

Trudgill, P. 2003 *A Glossary of Sociolinguistics* Edinburgh: Edinburgh University Press.

Wardhaugh, R. 2002 *An Introduction to Sociolinguistics* Fourth edition. Oxford: Blackwell.

Wassink, A.B. 1999 'Historic Low Prestige and Seeds of Change: Attitudes Toward Jamaican Creole.' *Language in Society* 28:57–92.

Webster's New International Dictionary [Webster's Third] 1961 New York: Merriam-Webster.

Wolfram, W. and Schilling-Estes, N. 1998 *American English* Oxford: Blackwell.

Wray, A., Trott, K. and Bloomer, A. 1998 *Projects in Linguistics: A Practical Guide to Researching Language* London: Arnold.

Yule, H. and Burnell, A.C. 1886 *Hobson-Jobson: The Anglo-Indian Dictionary* (1996 reprint of second edition 1902) Ware, Herts: Wordsworth Editions Ltd.

Yule, G. 1996 *The Study of Language* Second edition. Cambridge: Cambridge University Press.

Index